I0015058

ISBN: EBOOK   978-1-64873-205-8
ISBN Hardcover: 9781648732171
ISBN Paperback 978-1-64873-274-4

Printed in the United States of America
Published by: Writer's Publishing House
Prescott, Az 86301

Cover and Interior Design by Creative Artistic Excellence Marketing

Project Management and Book Launch by Creative Artistic Excellence Marketing lizzymcnett.com

IAuthor

Marketing Resource Guide

By Writer's Publishing House

(Lizzy McNett)

Table of Contents

Introduction

What is marketing? By definition, it is "the process or technique of promoting, selling, and distributing a product or service." But, the art of marketing is more than just assembling product lines or writing simplified phrases. The process takes time and dedication to assemble a unique campaign for each individual company or business.

Writer's Publishing House has developed an exceptional process; a marketing strategy grows out of a company's value proposition, by which the client's campaigns shine above the competition.

The best marketing campaigns are those that revolve around product solicitation. As an example, Walmart markets as a discount retailer with 'everyday low prices.' A company does not create a marketing strategy from scratch; they start with the value proposition and distill the campaign from those messages.

The basics behind 'IAuthor' is all about matching the customer's needs to the right product or services.

Proper marketing eliminates the struggle to find your potential customer. When a business owner creates content designed to address the consumer's needs it will attract qualified prospects, along with the ability to build trust-based on compatible interests.

A good marketing campaign is based on educating the potential customer. People do not want to be sold. The best option is to communicate through your knowledge and expertise in the field you practice. When a person understands a concept clearly, it is easy for them to make an informed decision.

In the IAuthor Marketing Resource Guide, readers will find a step-by-step process to develop exceptional marketing campaigns, ones that can compete with large companies who have fully staffed departments to spearhead all product marketing. Once the key fundamentals of social media networking and website basics are learned, professionally creating campaigns is highly simplified.

Understanding the Importance of Marketing

What Does Marketing Mean?

The term marketing entails many activities; however, all are associated with selling your company's products and services. The most obvious area of marketing is advertising, but consumer research should not be ignored. Marketing is all about matching the customer's needs to the right product or services. Proper marketing eliminates the struggle to find your potential customer. When a business owner creates content designed to address the consumer's needs, it will attract qualified prospects. It also generates the ability to build trust-based on compatible interests.

Although, one should never confuse marketing with sales. Yes, they are equally combined in the business world, but they have very distinctive functions. Solid marketing platforms serve as the enabler for sales, by transforming the potential customer into a long-standing client.

The marketing team must work closely to validate a strong advertising campaign based on the value at every stage of the customer's journey with your business. The method of attracting, engaging, and delighting consumers builds trust and helps to grow your company.

Some marketing strategies include these actions:

- Determine the type of product needed through consumer research, studying quantifying sales patterns of similar goods or services within your business qualifications.
- Modify the existing products or services to align with current marketing patterns.
- Analyze the best way to reach potential clients by making them aware of the products and services you offer.
- Design marketing campaigns based on the data you compiled.
- Confirm customer relationships using follow-up campaigns or loyalty programs.

A good marketing campaign is based on educating the potential customer. People do not want to be sold. The best option is to communicate through your knowledge and expertise in the field you practice. When a person understands a concept clearly, it is easy for them to make an informed decision.

I Don't Know What to Say on social media

Social media marketing is by far the most cost-effective targeting campaign available, but only when the business follows some simple guidelines. Not all platforms are a good fit for every business, which is why consumer research is so important. Once you have chosen the best platforms the next option is learning what to post and avoid pitfalls.

You might be wondering, "What do I say? Or how do I write a good post?" Let's discuss that topic for a moment.

Below are examples of what **Writer's Publishing House** recommends. Your post should pinpoint an objective: Begin the process with your objectives, then assess how you will achieve those goals.

Create your authority: Every business owner or manager must establish themselves as an authority figure in their field. Why should someone do business with you? What do you have to offer them?

Write posts to gain interaction: The best way to get free advertising with most social media platforms is to get likes and responses. As the response grows, so does the showing of your postings.

Confirm appreciation: social media is not a monologue for someone to boost their achievements. It will turn followers off. The objective is to interact in a meaningful way; people will know when a post is genuine or just bravado. The best way to show recognition to someone is to like, share, or respond.

Stand out from the rest: The purpose is to build a personal brand. It will convey a persona the public will learn to identify.

Set a goal: The action requires investment, both time and money. Determine exactly what you are trying to convey, then study the results. Statistics will show the outcome and your successes or failures.

Lead in one platform: Use consumer usage findings to target your aligned customer. Claim your profiles, but focus on just one at a time. Initially, start sharing other posts that pertain to the goals you set for yourself or business. As you gain recognition, then begin writing and developing a marketing campaign.

Create a social media calendar: Once you can plan your social media actions, you will gain consistency. It will generate higher results, and an outlook to the desired goals.

Use visual content: Most users have short attention spans and writing lengthy posts will yield unnoticed results. Instead, use photos of good quality and short videos.

Get some help: Small business owners are limited on time, and inconsistency will not improve the end game. Writer's Publishing House can be a valued partner in achieving successful social media marketing goals.

Social media marketing can seem impossible to master, especially if you are already tasked with all the affairs of running a small business. But you are not alone, and with the right guidance, anyone can be successful with social media.

Chapter One:

The Importance of Marketing Strategies

Breaking Down Marketing Strategy

Marketing strategies are often confused with marketing plans. Because they do feed off one another, it is not unusual to find the marketing strategy and the marketing plan baked together into a single document. Although the transition between the two is blurry, a marketing strategy covers the big picture of what the business offers: the value proposition and related brand messaging. The marketing plan is how the business will get across the key message: the platforms, the creative, the timing, and so on. The marketing strategy may also be absorbed upwards into corporate value statements and other strategy documents.

The Creation of a Marketing Strategy

A marketing strategy grows out of a company's value proposition. The value proposition summarizes the competitive advantage a company has in its market. The value proposition usually provides a key message for all marketing. Walmart, for example, is a discount retailer with "everyday low prices," and its business operations and marketing revolve around that. A company is never creating a marketing strategy from scratch; they start with the value proposition and distill the key marketing message(s) from that.

Once the value proposition is succinctly stated, the hard work is done. Any marketing asset, from a print ad design to a social media campaign, can be judged by how well it communicates the value proposition. To further the efficiency of marketing efforts, market research can be added to the marketing strategy to identify untapped audiences or refine the target consumer. Finally, an overall goal for the marketing strategy can be set, with all the subsequent marketing plans inheriting the responsibility for delivering on it. These can be concrete, bottom-line goals such as increasing sales or something less direct like climbing the ranking of trusted providers within the industry.

Marketing plans are operational documents that get more attention because they are the day-to-day work that a company does to sell itself to the world. That said, a marketing plan would be meaningless without a message, a target market, and a goal — the core of every marketing strategy.

It takes a lot of time and effort to develop and maintain a marketing campaign that resonates with your intended audience. As a strategic thinker, however, the development of a marketing campaign takes even more consideration. After all, we're always searching for ways to gain the oh-so-important competitive edge.

There are times, though, when we all hit the proverbial wall. If you find yourself in that situation, then you may want to check out these fifteen marketing strategies that will spark your creative energy.

1) Partner with allies.

Marketing partnerships have several benefits to push a marketing campaign. For starters, when you collaborate with someone else, you tend to deliver better content. On top of that, marketing partnerships are cheaper to create, see success more quickly, and expose your brand to a new audience.

For example, before being acquired by eBay, Half.com convinced the town of Halfway, Oregon, to change its name to Half.com in exchange for stock, Internet access, and other giveaways. The tactic gained a lot of attention to the textbook rental company. Another example was when Converse teamed up with Guitar Center to record music entitled "Rubber Tracks." The content was then used to create a series of YouTube videos that focused on the musicians.

2) Embrace user-generated content.

According to a survey of 839 millennials, they spend "5.4 hours a day with content created by their peers. This represents 30 percent of their total media time and is rivaled only by all traditional media types combined (print, radio, and television, at 33 percent)." In the same survey, "Millennials reported that UGC is 20 percent more influential on their purchase decisions than other media."

You can achieve this by having customers share personal stories (Estee Lauder's international breast cancer action campaign), exchange ideas (Salesforce's Idea Exchange), and by giving them the tools to make an ad for you (Nissan's VersaVid campaign that was shared on Instagram and Vine) or through humor (Doritos Roulette bags).

3) Collaborate with influencers.

Another way to gain a new audience and extend brand awareness is by collaborating with the top influencers in your industry. The home improvement store Lowe's allowed "top designers and mom bloggers to take over its Instagram account for a few days at a time." By allowing these influencers to share inspirational content, Lowe's was able to tap into a new audience.

4) Help customers solve a problem.

As perfectly stated on HubSpot, "You're in business because you provide solutions." Some of the ways you can help customers solve a problem are by creating how-to content, offering exclusives that make their lives easier, listening/responding to them or creating apps/tools.

You could also create a campaign as Orca Chevrolet did in Brazil. The company partnered with a local tow company and rescued stranded drivers by arriving in the new Orca. Not only did Chevy save the day, but it also gave drivers a chance to test drive the car.

5) Let customers interact.

No matter the product or service you're offering, your customers want to interact with your company, or at least other customers. AMC, for example, created an online tool that allowed you to Mad Man Yourself. American Express connects small business owners and helpful resources through its OPEN Forum.

6) Experiment with new channels and platforms.

Don't hesitate to try out new channels and platforms to promote your brand. As Clare McDermott, editor of Chief Content Officer magazine and owner of SoloPortfolio points out on the Content Marketing Institute, the Four Seasons introduced the Pin.Pack. Go program on Pinterest. This was an industry-first campaign that allowed guests to co-curate a customer travel itinerary through a Pinterest board.

7) Take a bite out of Apple.

Apple deserves special mention mainly because it's a brand that has created an entire generation of lifelong advocates. How did they accomplish this? Remember when the iPod was introduced? Apple's now-iconic strategy involved empathy, focus, and impute when they used silhouettes of people enjoying the iPod. It may not have been the best MP3 player, but it created brand recognition that helped dominate the market.

8) Have some fun.

You probably never heard of Dollar Shave Club until the company released that humorous YouTube video. The company continues to have its way with the shaving industry. Taco Bell and Old Spice are other examples of companies that are having fun with their marketing campaigns. Even campaigns you wouldn't expect are getting in on the action.

Caterpillar launched its "Built for It" campaign by having five Cat construction machines playing a giant game of Jenga.

9) Get employees involved.

Let employees be your biggest champions and brand advocates. That's what happened with Caterpillar's "Built for It" campaign. The videos tapped into the allegiance of the brand, which motivated them to share the videos with friends and family.

10) Be a little weird.

You don't always have to play it safe. Sometimes you want to think outside of the box and get a little weird. For example, to help launch the new radio station FM 96.3 in Glasgow, Scotland, the station placed empty guitar racks throughout the city. The hook? Each rack had a sign that read: "Free Air Guitar. Take One." It was unique and matched the brand perfectly - who hasn't played a little air guitar when listening to the radio?

11) Don't forget about the existing customers.

It is important to obtain new customers if you want your business to grow, but don't forget about the customers you already have. As Belle Beth Cooper notes on the Buffer Blog, you could use the "upside-down funnel" approach. This could include making customers feel like they're part of an exclusive club, giving them something extra, and making them feel like VIPs.

12) Use big data to target customers.

Big data is now helping retailers target specific customers. Red Roof Inn uses canceled flight information to send messages to stranded travelers. A pizza chain uses data to send out coupons to customers who are experiencing bad weather or power outages. In short, big data can be used to predict purchasing trends. With this information, you can get in touch with consumers before they search for your products or services.

13) Venture into the concrete jungle.

You can still do a little offline marketing to create a buzz surrounding your product or service. For example, you could hire an artist to paint a mural (with permission, of course). You could also go the route of Citi Bike. Having bicyclists riding around with your logo or name is a clever way to grab attention. Another great example was when the Copenhagen Zoo shrink-wrapped city buses so that it appeared that they were squeezed by a giant boa constrictor.

14) Tap into nostalgia.

Entrepreneur magazine shared an interesting discovery from the Journal of Consumer Research. The study found "that people who were asked to think about the past were willing to pay more for products than those who were asked to think about new or future memories; another experiment showed an increased willingness to give more money to others after recalling a nostalgic event." Maybe that's why brands like Coca-Cola, Calvin Klein, and Internet Explorer have launched campaigns that take Millennials back to the 90s.

15) Tell a cross-media story.

Storytelling is one of the most effective methods of marketing. But how do you modernize it? Axe's "Susan Glenn" is a perfect example of a modern story that was shared across various media platforms. If you don't recall, Axe tapped into the memories of the girl who got away. Instead of just repacking the content, the story was told differently on different channels. There was also a 60-second film, an interactive billboard at Times Square, and unbranded memes.

Section One:

Marketing Strategy Definitions

Marketing strategies are used by businesses to promote their products and services. Let's have a look at the proper definition.

Marketing Strategy Definition

Marketing strategy is used by different companies to collaborate with their consumers. It is also employed to notify the customers about the features, specifications, and benefits of the company's products. It is focused on encouraging a target population to buy those specific products and services. The marketing strategies might be innovative or they can be previously tried or tested strategies. Effective marketing strategies help a company get ahead of the competition. They might be innovative or they can be previously tried or tested strategies.

Points to Ponder for Marketing

There are different types of marketing strategies available. You have to pick one as per your business requirements. Before choosing the right marketing strategy for your business, consider the following points.

1) Define the target population.

Defining the target population is the main and most necessary step in choosing your marketing strategy. It gives the proper demographics which helps in selecting the most appropriate marketing plan for your business.

2) Test your audience.

Create a hypothetical process of buying to test your audience. Once you know the buying behavior of your target audience, you can select a more appropriate marketing strategy.

3) Consider marketing strategies.

Once you know the demographics - their knowledge, attitudes, and behaviors - you can select a more appropriate marketing strategy.

4) Evaluate those strategies.

Once you have considered the marketing strategies and found the applicable ones, asses them, apply them, and evaluate them. This process must be for testing purposes and the most suitable and productive strategy must be applied.

Types of Marketing Strategies

There are different types of marketing strategies available. Picking up a marketing strategy includes analyzing the needs of your business, your target audience, and the specifications of your products.

The two main types of marketing strategy are:
Business to business (B2B) is the marketing of products to businesses or other organizations for use in the production of goods, for use in general business operations (such as office supplies), or resale to other consumers (such as a wholesaler selling to a retailer).

Business to consumer (B2C) marketing refers to the process of selling products and services directly between consumers who are the end-users of its products or services. Most companies that sell directly to consumers can be referred to as B2C companies

The most common form of marketing is business to consumer (B2C) marketing. Let's explore a bit more.

The following are the different types of marketing strategies available.

1) Paid advertising

This includes multiple approaches for marketing. It includes traditional approaches like TVCs and print media advertising. Also, one of the most well-known marketing approaches is internet marketing. It includes various methods like PPC (pay per click) and paid advertising.

2) Cause marketing

Cause marketing links the services and products of a company to a social cause or issue. It is also well known as cause-related marketing.

3) Relationship marketing

This type of marketing is focused on customer building, enhancing existing relationships with customers, and improving customer loyalty.

4) Undercover marketing

This type of marketing strategy focuses on marketing the product while customers remain unaware of the marketing strategy. It is also known as stealth marketing.

5) Word of mouth

This type relies on what impression you leave on people. It is traditionally the most important type of marketing strategy. Being heard is important in the business world. When you give quality services to customers, they'll likely promote you.

6) Internet marketing

This type is also known as cloud marketing. It usually happens over the Internet. All the marketing items are shared on the Internet and promoted on various platforms via multiple approaches.

7) Transactional marketing

Sales are particularly the most challenging work. Even for the largest retailers, selling is always tough, especially when there are high volume targets. However, with the new marketing strategies, selling isn't as difficult as it was. In transactional marketing, retailers encourage customers to buy with shopping coupons, discounts, and huge events. It increases the chances of sales and motivates the target audience to buy the promoted products.

8) Diversity marketing

This type caters to a diverse audience by customizing and integrating different marketing strategies. It covers different aspects like culture, beliefs, attitudes, views, and other specific needs.

9) Brand marketing

Companies, businesses, or individuals must always be observant of their public reputation. An online presence is important, but making sure the content is favorable is essential. This is why brand marketing is advantageous. The idea behind this method is to create content based on client testimonials. The concept most likely will not improve search results; nonetheless, it does have a positive impact on brand image. Beware, however, that when consumers research the brand, the results must be constructive. Any negative feedback will be detrimental. Do not mistake this kind of marketing for brand management, that is a whole other segment of business maintenance.

In Conclusion

Marketing strategies have made it much easier to promote products and services. They also limit the strategy to the target audience ensuring the proper advancement of the business.

Chapter Two:

What are Hashtags?

Remember the old days when symbols were something you used on a typewriter or dialed on a phone? Now with social media and the invention of smartphones, it has brought about a whole new meaning to communication. Today when using any social media platform, it's impossible to escape using some type of symbols like hashtags or emoticons. But in this section, we will be discussing just hashtags.

It's not surprising that you may be unfamiliar with how to use, or the meaning of, a hashtag. It's a relatively new concept unless you're part of the younger generation. We all know how our children migrate to electronics.

Once we explain "what" a hashtag is, you will most likely know "how" to use them. At first glance, the use of hashtags might seem confusing. But it's a powerful marking tool to engage your audience with literally no cost.

The concept started because of the demanding competition within social media platforms. If you want to stand out from the crowd, the user must create a unique approach to having their post seen. Hence, the reason for hashtags and emoticons. "The specific definition of the hashtag is a keyword or phrase preceded by the hash symbol (#), written within a post or comment to highlight and facilitate a search," WIXBlog.com. The idea is that the post can be indexed by the social network for anyone to locate even if they are not one of your followers. By increasing impressions, you essentially improve marketing goals.

With the use of hashtags, your social contacts are expanded to more than just your followers. Think of this as content-based marketing, similar to shopping on Amazon where it shows you recommended products in the same category as what you have chosen. It has the potential of reaching thousands of more users that could lead to customers or new followers.

One concept that must be observed: It can be tempting to use a simple word like #write, but with millions of posts each day, the chances of it being noticed are small. A better option would be a more specific hashtag such as #lovewriting. It will allow you to follow specific hashtags and people with similar interests. Give the tag some thought before posting.

Hashtags Have Three Categories

Content hashtags: As the title dictates, content hashtags pertain to your expertise, product, or service. They have the potential to greatly expand your brand.

Trending hashtags: A great way to capitalize on boosting your brand is using popular hashtags. But use caution; remember to analyze the word ahead of time and ask, "Will this tag increase my brand, or get lost in the millions of other posts each day?" The best trending hashtags are the ones that go viral; random moments about something funny, holidays, or spur of the moment thoughts.

Brand-specific hashtags: If you choose to use a prevalent or generic hashtag, the posts may be lost in the shuffle. It's a good idea to create a unique word and be consistent. One great way to expand your brand is to get users to engage with incentives like discounts or free products. Plus, you can always test different hashtags to find out which ones get the best response, and no one is saying you must use only one hashtag.

One last word of caution: do not go overboard. Using hashtags to write an entire caption can defeat your agenda. Each channel has a specific number of hashtags allowed in each post. The last suggestion, only put the hashtag next to a word with the most significance.

According to buffer social media research shows the best results on each one of these three channels. Below are a few of the top social site results:

- Twitter: One to two #s
- Instagram: up to eleven #s
- Facebook: Not recommended

Twitter

Hashtagging on Twitter can have a major impact when it comes to follower count. It can be used with general and/or non-specific hashtags. If general hashtag words are used that are prominent, such as #creative, #events, #TIFF, it is more likely that tweets will reach beyond your follower list.

Twitter hashtags encourage people to take part in conversations with the same topic, and users to engage with one another even if they are not following each other. While hashtagging on Twitter can help social media presence, using long and wordy hashtags, like #bestcoffeeshopintheworld, in a Tweet can damage your presence, as hashtags are used to increase search results and engage with others. In addition to long hashtags, using too many hashtags in one post can also be harmful to social media presence. If the tweet is filled with more hashtags than content, it will provide evidence that the business or individual is desperate and certainly dilutes the message being conveyed.

Instagram

As with Twitter, using hashtags on Instagram can help engagement with more than just your followers. Hashtags on Instagram give "audiences an organic way to discover branded content through the topics and forums that interest them," according to Jenna MacDonald. Community engagement is a good way to build a brand, whereas hashtags allow users to find specific members of the community to interact with. The main concept is to increase presence on social media through other avenues besides gaining followers (MacDonald, 2017).

Instagram hashtags can assist with building a bigger audience. A great way to expand your presence is using the same hashtags of the audience that is interacting with your posts or to follow the same topics. Avoid using hashtags on photos; they function better added to the input section while creating the post.

Facebook and LinkedIn

It is a common misbelief that hashtags should be used on every platform, but that is not the case. As an example, hashtags are less effective on Facebook or LinkedIn. The hashtag will not be clickable on LinkedIn, and Facebook posts just perform better without hashtags. Facebook originally introduced them in 2013, however, research shows they do not pose a benefit. In fact, many times, analytics show they are an irritant to users.

In conclusion, if you have not chosen to use hashtags on social media posts it may be time to put the action to good use. The use of hashtags seems to be a growing craze that could benefit any business, company, or individual looking to improve their online presence.

Chapter Three:

Social Media and Email Marketing make great partners

As social media continues to progress and become more popular around the globe, some businesses think email marketing has fallen by the wayside. But, it's just the opposite. According to Neil Patel, 85% of adult internet users have and use email regularly. That outranks surfing the web and social media which shows only 17%. Now, imagine if you combined the two marketing options? Anytime a business owner can intermingle marketing strategies with a cross-platform, their results will improve dramatically.

The number of consumers that make buying choices based on a single medium is limited. Therefore, marketers should never focus all their time on one channel. Multiple advertising options correlate with buyers' natural rhythms. So, let's talk about how you can combine multiple mediums to improve business and reach a greater audience.

Shareaholic states, "Facebook is the number one referral traffic source for websites." Websites like Buzzfeed get most of their website traffic from social media.

But, for the marketing plan to work, you must continue using both outlets equally. The strategies remain the same: quality tagline, magnetic subject lines, etc.

If you're a business owner, chances are you've already considered using social media marketing to help get the word out about your business.

In fact, many small business owners are using sites like Facebook, Twitter, LinkedIn, Pinterest, and Instagram to help grow their businesses. And if you are still standing on the social sidelines, there's never been a better time to get started.

Below are ten reasons social media marketing could benefit any business, company, or individual, according to Constant Contact.

1) **Social media helps get the word out:** First and foremost — social media does, in fact, help get the word out about your business.

But even more important than the exposure, it provides you with the opportunity to grow relationships with your target audience. Your fans, followers, and connections are people who know your organization, have likely done business with you in the past, and will be most likely to tell their friends about you.

2) **Social media is popular:** You don't need to be a dedicated reader of tech blogs or an expert in online marketing to know that social media is popular among consumers.

According to the Pew Research Center, 69 percent of American adults use social networks, which means that social media will touch nearly every customer that walks through your door.

For most small businesses, Facebook — which has 2.32 billion monthly active users — is the jumping-off point for getting started with social media marketing.

With its extensive reach and dynamic functionality, there are very few businesses that couldn't benefit from having a presence on Facebook. And starting there will make it easier when you want to try something new.

3) **Social media is cost-effective:** As more social networks add algorithms that filter what users see in their news feeds, your organic content may get lost in the shuffle. Take advantage of the low-cost advertising features offered by social networks to promote your content and special offers.

Most social media advertising is cheaper than traditional advertising, so you don't have to spend a lot of money to reach more people, increase your audience, and grow your business.

The next section will show business owners how to leverage these two channels to improve audience impressions.

4) **Social media reaches all ages and demographics:** social media defies age barriers. A Pew Research Center study found that 69 percent of US adults are using social networks.

While much of that percentage is between 18-29, a substantial amount is attributed to other ages that use social media as well, including 34% of Americans 65 and older. So, no matter how young or old your target audience may be, chances are most of them are already logging on and waiting for you to get started.

5) **Social media encourages two-way communication:** social media gives you the power to learn more about your audience, their interests, and collect feedback.

Ask your customers to share their thoughts, questions, and ideas to get to know them better. You can respond just as fast, without having to pick up the phone or worry the customer isn't seeing your response.

6) **Social media users are active**: One thing you have to know about social media users is that when they say they are on social media; they are really on social media.

Social media users in the US check their accounts 17 times a day, according to an Informate Mobile Intelligence report. While a customer may visit your store once a week, they could see your social media posts in their feed multiple times during the week.

7) **Social media lets you share A LOT about your business:** social media sites are becoming the go-to place for consumers who want to learn more about a business. That's because these sites allow businesses to offer the most up-to-date information about anything from products, services, or upcoming events.

Also, much of your activity and profiles on social media sites can be made public, meaning they can be indexed by search engines — one more way to make sure your business or organization comes up as the answer when someone is searching for a solution to a problem.

8) **Social media is perfect for customer service:** Providing stellar customer service is likely already a top priority for your small business. But along with the two-way communication that social media provides, it also offers a unique opportunity to step up your customer service game and provide instant gratification to your target audience.

This will allow you to showcase just how much you care about providing a memorable experience and will ensure that no customer inquiry goes unnoticed. And by monitoring social media for customer feedback and offering a response, you can drive real business results. Businesses that engage with customer service requests via social media earn 20-40 percent more revenue per customer, according to Bain and Company.

9) **Social media can make a big difference for your email marketing:** social media has

completely changed the game when it comes to how small businesses think of email marketing. Sharing your email newsletter across your social networks can open your content up to a whole new audience and generate the type of buzz you've been looking for.

Not only that, but you can also use sites like Facebook to attract more readers by including a Join My Mailing List link right on your page.

Together, these two powerful tools have reshaped the marketing landscape and have leveled the playing field for small businesses trying to better connect with current customers and reach new audiences for their business.

10) Social media is everywhere: Today, more than half of all Americans are smartphone users, and more and more businesses are offering mobile-friendly experiences. The benefit of the increased presence of mobile activity in our daily lives is huge for small businesses.

Most major social networks, including Facebook, Twitter, Pinterest, and Instagram, offer free mobile apps that let business owners manage their presence on-the-go.

More importantly, these apps let customers connect to their favorite sites wherever they are. These users aren't just sharing updates from their own lives, they're searching for businesses, products, and services, and connecting with brands through their social channels.

Having a social media presence that's accessible via mobile can improve the chances of your business getting found when someone is searching for a place to eat or a product to buy while on-the-go (Collier, 2019).

Writer's Publishing House Social Media Marketing's favorite email resource is Constant Contact.

According to a Constant Contact survey, small businesses that use multiple channels in conjunction with email reported: more customer engagement (73 percent), more new customers (57 percent), more website traffic (54 percent), more revenue (40 percent), and more referrals (39 percent).

We have a special link for a free 60-day trial

Social media and email marketing are a team meant to benefit each other.

Connecting with your customers on Facebook, Twitter, Instagram, and other major social media channels is a great way to build relationships and raise awareness for your business. But the real power of social media comes from integrating it with your other marketing channels — like email marketing.

1) **Put a brand before the subscriber:** Upload your subscriber list on all major social media sites. The consumer can see your business in a real-time setting. One of the biggest challenges a company faces is building trust with their clients. When subscribers can interact with your business in a social setting, it improves brand image. Then, make sure your posts are solving a pain problem. How can your company help with an issue?

2) **Social media can grow an email list:** Lead generations can increase a subscriber list. Ads can be sent to users who've sent a message to your Facebook page within the last year. Collect the email and you can follow-up later to

see if they have received your message and whether they are interested in your product.

3) **Connect with your subscribers on social media:** Once you have uploaded your subscriber list to the major social media sites, it's important to connect with them. A few ways to interact might be:

- Contact about missed messages in their Inbox.
- Re-connect with subscribers who stopped opening emails.
- Follow-up on future sales, or assist to help complete a project.
  - Plan a sale for specific groups of people, who like your company, or potential clients.

4) **Test email marketing strategies on social media:** The best way to get an idea of your marketing plan is to run some trials. When you have determined the response, adjust accordingly to increase response. Once you are satisfied with the outcome, create an email blast.

Marketing can be challenging, but it is a necessary evil that cannot be ignored. Below are some resources to help you with this task:

- Social Share: promote emails on social media
- Use Social Buttons: it makes it easier for contacts to locate your pages. When creating any post, make sure users can contact your business easily. Provide a direct link.
- Grow Your List: social media can be used to gather the names directly into your contact list

- Social Media Calendars: The best way to improve a social media presence is to use a schedule calendar
- Create Posta from Email Blasts: Posts will appear on social platforms and educate followers. When users click the post, it takes them directly to the email.
- Invite Contacts to Your Facebook Page
- Add a Sign-up Form to Your Facebook Page

Marketing any business has its challenges under the best of circumstances. But with commitment, strategy, and planning, the process is much simpler. One of the best practices is to study the market and learn your type of client. Then, focus your energy on reaching that type of consumer. Remember, whatever you focus on grows, either good or bad. People can read and feel the intentions behind your marketing, so keep it honest.

Chapter Four:

Facebook Business Fan Pages

If you don't know the importance of a business Facebook page, you have not studied statistics. In fact, more than 2 billion active monthly users are visible on the social media platform. The stats speak for themselves. But, marketing on Facebook is something that should be planned, and ultimately you must clearly understand the mechanics of the platform. It is a tricky science to maintain a constant presence on the social media outlet.

According to Forbes, if you have a following of 1,000 Facebook fans only 5% to10% will see your regular posts. Those numbers may not sound appealing, which is why it's imperative to have an active presence. Let's explore some options to improve the success of any business Facebook page.

1) **Why:** Should my business be on Facebook? All businesses don't need to have a Facebook presence.
2) **What:** Determine your goals.
    - Improve brand awareness

- Build a following
- Present your expertise
- Extend your cliental
- Form new partnerships
- Increase sales or prospective leads

3) Who: What is your target audience? The more you know about your specific clients the better.

4) How: Create a strategic plan. Remember, strategies are never written in stone, they are meant to change and adapt.

The next section is just as important. Facebook allows a specific amount of space for every user. Businesses will want to pay attention to their cover and profile images and about section.

- Cover images are 851 pixels by 315 pixels.
- Profile images are 180 pixels by 180 pixels (visual is 160x160).
- About section is under the profile and allows for 155 characters. If you can list your website that is very important.

Cover Images: Before you add a cover picture, make sure it represents the description of your business. This section must be considered prime real estate.

Optimized Posting: Posting regularity is a commonly asked question, so you are not alone. Random posting on a personal page is alright, but will not work on a business page, nor will over posting. You must find a pattern that works for the business. Study the statics and optimize engagement. The best option is creating a social media calendar such as Hoote Suite, Postcorn, or Zoho, along with many others.

Learning the Platform: Facebook is powerful but complicated. One statistic you may not be aware of, less than 16% of followers see the postings. Some formulas:

- Attraction: This measurement determines the connection between the viewing user and the story author. The lower the number the higher the score.
- Weight: Postings carry different emphases (videos, photos, links, etc.).
- Time-lapse: All postings lose appeal over time.

Business Page Specifics: Businesses are open to public search engines. The page can be integrated with custom tabs to engage the audience, and you can have as many followers as you like.

Comment Responses: This section is imperative to expand your social media presence. Users should respond to all comments and make sure people can post on your page or send private messages.

Promote on Multiple Platforms: If you want to increase visibility, then link your page with the business page. The option may be nerve-racking, but you can always create a public personal page and maintain your privacy away from work. Access the advantages of other social media outlets, like Twitter, Instagram, LinkedIn, Alignable, and many others.

Participate in Your Page: Recent result have shown that just using Facebook ads are not enough to build a following. While the ads will increase likes, visibility, engagement, events, or improve your brands, they are not a one-stop-shop. Use the following:

- Promoted posts
- Sponsored stories
- Facebook ads
- Offers

Content Value: If you have not heard of the 80/20 rule of business it's very effective. Post 80% original content, something that provides value to potential clients, and 20% promotional content. People do not want to be sold or have someone pushing sales in their faces. It's a sure way to turn off new customers. The content and quality of your page will sell the consumer.

Pertinent Content: Post and comment on products or services that relate to your business. Too often people post random topics that do not correlate with their business. Company websites and social media pages should be about your business. They should include key points: Who are you? Why should they care? And what can you do for them? Some topics for business pages include:

- Receive discounts or promotions (FREE giveaway)
- Stay informed
- Be entertaining
- Interact and connect
- Educate the consumer
- Be supportive

Conclusion: The options for marketing are endless, but whatever you decide it must be informative without being spammy. Below are 9 types of marketing posts everyone should be using.

- Inspirational Quotes
- Memes or GIFs
- Educational, Interesting, and Funny Videos (Video is HOT! HOT! HOT!)
- Life Hack Posts (Simplify Life Options)
- Call to Action Buttons/Options

Section Two:

Facebooks Advertising

In the world of advertising, there are many stand-out agencies, but no one business is going to be the perfect fit for every person or company. The important factor, in this case, is choosing the agency that fits your needs the best. A few steps are necessary to find the right agency:

- Ask questions that pertain to your needs
- Ask for references and client testimonials

Search and review the company online.

- How does the website appear, and do they have a good reputation?
- Be comfortable with the agent assigned to your account.

Remember, you are the client, but make sure the person you are dealing with is knowledgeable in the field of FB advertising.

Lastly, customer service is the key to any good business. Make sure the company is legitimately concerned about your advertising needs and you are not just a financial number.

Facebook has become an incredible marketing outlet for many companies. However, it can be an expensive mistake if your ads are not designed and presented properly. It is a harsh reality; very few individuals run effective Facebook ads.

While Facebook has a massive potential to grow your business, some big mistakes must be avoided. Below we will review some of those mistakes.

Why Advertise on Facebook?

While the social media platform was originally designed as a place where people from all over the world could connect, keep in touch with long-lost loved ones, or meet the perfect mate and many other opportunities, is has become much more.

If you are still questioning, the option, consider this: Facebook has over 2.23 billion monthly users as of 12/31/2018 (according to Zephoria Marketing). That's one-quarter of the Earth's population. Approximately 93 % of those users are on a mobile device. The average person spends nearly an hour a day on Facebook. In this case, the numbers speak for themselves.

Facebook Benefits Above Paid Ads

1. Virtual Potential

    - Sharing ads
    - Ad commenting
    - More attention means additional branding potential

Facebook Ad Targeting

As you create an ad on Facebook, you will be asked to designate a target audience. This is the data people voluntarily provide.

- User profiles
- Posting comments
- Likes
- Shares
- Groups
- Photos
- Liked pages
- Events
- And much more…

All these factors seem amazing, but without the proper data and campaign clarity, your ads will not be successful. Below are some mistakes that many marketers fail to learn.

- Not being compliant
- Failure to measure ROI (Return on Investment)
- Ineffective targeting
- Boring copy
  - Uninteresting images
  - Lack of funnel clarity
  - No re-targeting

To have a successful Facebook ad, some critical aspects must be applied.

The next phase of preparing a Facebook ad is optimization. Facebook ads require more than creating a "Facebook Pixel or an Audience." Therefore, the best way to succeed is to initiate Optimization Hacks. What is an Optimization Hack, you ask?

Most people think of hacking as a four-letter word, but in this case, it describes the methods used to drive major amounts of traffic to your Facebook page, website, or business digital outlet. The term comes from Conversion Sciences.

"Conversion rate optimization is a systematic process of increasing the percentage of your website's visitors that take the desired action on a certain page. This includes optimizing the landing pages and the website overall, using real-time analytics, tested design, and psychological elements, to turn your website, visitors, into customers. Don't make a rookie mistake! Not every one of these 'hacks' will work for your website."

Once optimized, the idea is that your campaign will improve as a result. Below is a list of Facebook optimization hacks to help improve ad results. Start with these items:

- Improve ad click-through rate
- Lower ad cost
- Extend ROI audience
- Decrease cost-per-acquisition
- Improve sales with the same budget

Successful marketing is only accomplished with constant attention. It requires the alteration of your ads to remain high yielding. The next section lists the most beneficial optimization hacks.

- Optimize likes and shares
- Use the most successful campaigns (ads with the best results)
- Set an ad schedule to reach the biggest audience
- Work to improve ad fatigue and rotation
- Alter ad placement
- Run A/B ads to test ideas
- Vary the dynamics of your ads dramatically
- Pick the correct campaign objective
- Delete converted ads from the targeted audience
- Create auto-optimization rules

The conclusion is, Facebook advertising is a continual process and will never be perfect; a black and white approach will not work. These guidelines will help improve resources over the long haul. Successful marketing takes time and consistency.

Chapter Five:

Using Twitter

Twitter is one of the fastest-paced social media platforms on the Internet, and the average shelf life for a post is 18 minutes (Neil Patel). The demographics are based on the younger generation with 313 million monthly active users.

As with any marketing plan, it's about more than just posting on occasion when your business has a new product or sale to promote. Successful networkers engage their audience and interact with them regularly, not just push product sales. Twitter marketing can be powerful if used properly.

The key to understanding Twitter is the revolving speed of posting. Tweets move 4x times faster than posts on Facebook, which makes it imperative you act accordingly. All tweets must pack a powerful punch to be effective. But not to worry; below are some steps to help create valuable ad copy for tweeting.

1) Pick a Twitter handle that is short, easy to remember, and correlates with your brand.

a. When someone searches your name, they will use the handle to locate your profile. For example: Instead of using the full business name shorten it to @ (your initials, or business initials).

b. Short Twitter names are more likely to get a response.

c. Brands and logos are a must for a successful marketing plan.

    i. Photos or logos need to be clean and professional. **Remember**, this is the image of your business.

d. The header or banner is where you can get creative. Design a simple but elegant message about your business.

e. **Do not** change your handle, as people may get confused.

One word of caution: Once you start interacting with people on a social media platform, you must keep a close eye on replies and new messages. Potential clients will be more likely to connect with you there than in person or on the phone and email.

2) Optimize a business or personal bio: On Twitter, you have 160-characters to stage your info. It must blow the competitors away.

   a. Simple content: Who am I? What do I do? Provide information on the company and when it was founded.

      i. Keep info current and accurate

      ii. Add some life and passion for what you do

      iii. Boost a bit, but don't be too flamboyant

      iv. Target the information

      v. Use your tagline

3) Tweet during peak hours:

   a. Add relevant hashtags, it allows people to find your account while searching for specific products.

   b. Tag other brands that are associated with your unique business.

   c. Believe it or not, certain days of the week and times users are more active. When using Twitter, it's imperative to know the peak hours. Posting during peak hours will increase impressions, boost engagement, and add clicks.

According to Buffer, posts on Friday, Saturday, and Sunday stand a greater chance of being seen than those submitted during the week. Some studies have shown that posting from 12 pm to 6 pm yields the best results. If you post on the weekdays, the best hours are 12 pm to 3 pm. However, be sure to study the best times for your business, as they will vary. Once you have analyzed the best time, set your social calendar to post the prewritten material or pics. However, it's not an exact science and you must stay on top of the results.

How to Tweet

Once you are logged into Twitter, the tweet button appears in the top right corner of the page. By pressing the button, a box pops up for you to enter your text. There are four boxes on the bottom left of the box that allows you to, in this order, add photos/video, add a GIF, add a poll, or add a location.

At the bottom of the page is a plus sign, which allows the user to add another tweet to your previous tweet, creating a thread completely before having to post an original tweet. The emoticon on the middle right lets you add Emojis to the tweet.

Underneath the circle is the warning about your character limit. Only 280 characters are allowed. If you reach or exceed the limit, it will show you how many characters you'll need to cut out.

Creating Tweets

When a user tweets (creates posts) the results are shown to followers. However, if your profile is not public no one will see them except you. Following people grants access to their newsfeed on your profile. Although, that does not mean they will follow you back. You will typically be notified if they follow you back.

Twitter Newsfeed

The newsfeed is a compilation of all your posts in chronological order. Twitter feeds contain tweets from the people you follow and whatever has been retweeted. As your followers grow, so will the types of posts that appear. However, as you increase your follower list, it decreases the number of impressions on your tweets.

Twitter Threads

The thread is the string of tweets relating to the same topic. It is created by replying to the previous tweet. They allow users to communicate with longer messages despite the character limit.

Retweets

Retweets are when someone likes a post and reposts it on their page. Or, the person thinks it is an important topic.

Quote Tweets

These are when someone uses a quote within their community and then attaches a comment of their own. The commentary explains why you felt the post was important.

Twitter Trending

In addition to the newsfeed, Twitter offers an explore, or trending, page. The thread is created when many people tweet or hashtag on the same topic and it becomes a trending topic.

On renowned events such as the Oscars or the Superbowl, Twitter sets up an official tag that people can use. Users can click on the hashtag to see what else is being discussed. It is a wider glimpse of world events.

Direct Message

Twitter calls messaging someone a direct message, or DI. This is similar to using messenger or email, only it's set up on social media.

Twitter Election Labels

Twitter recently introduced what is called election labels. They are for users planning to vote in U.S. elections. Under the politician's name is a label and what seat they are running for, whether that is state governor, the US Senate, or the US House of Representatives.

Following and Unfollowing Others

The ability to follow or unfollow people is how you develop an interesting newsfeed. If you're on a desktop, go to other users' profiles and look for the follow button just beneath their header.

When you click it, the follow button will change from follow to following, or vice-versa. People's profiles will tell you the history if you have been connected to them at one time.

For those people who may post things the user may not want to see, muting is an option without unfollowing that person. For example, if someone is posting dessert recipes and it is the last thing you want to see, click 'mute@username.'

The user also has the option to block someone if they are being harassed or find the person disturbing. In this case, you can't see them and they can't see you.

What are Twitter Moments?

If a tweet reaches momentous results, like an awards show or sporting event, the social media platform creates Twitter Moments. It is a collection of tweets about a topic or event. The post can be tweeted, liked, pinned, and embedded like normal tweets, and when a user taps on the Moment it shows the collection of information. Moments are published with a cover photo and introduction, likening them to a "best of" compilation article.

Twitter developed Moments categorized under the following interest areas: News, Sports, Entertainment, and Fun.

Moments are available on a mobile device or desktop. On a desktop, you can find Twitter Moments by tapping the lightning bolt icon – it's in the top-left corner of Twitter on your browser

The button highlighted in red above will bring you to your Twitter Moments feed, where you can shuffle between five Moments categories across the top: News, Sports, Entertainment, Fun, and Today.

Twitter Moments on Mobile

If you are on a mobile device, Moments can be found by tapping the magnifying glass icon. The button will direct the user to the Explore tab, and you can shuffle between Twitter Moments sorted into News, Sports, Fun, or Entertainment across the top.

Chapter Six:

Using Pinterest

Pinterest is a relatively new social platform that is showing very promising results for over 70 million people marketing their products. It can combine new potential, making it extremely fun while adding value to your marketing plans.

As with any platform, Pinterest may not be ideal for your company, but it's well worth the effort and studying the results. A great way to gain new ideas and perspective is learning how some of the bigger companies market their products. Listed below are several techniques to combine with your posting calendar:

1. Pin at least 5x per day
2. Use a social media calendar
3. Apply for Rich Pins to add on your website or blog
4. Create "Pin It for Later" links

5. Post only properly sized images
6. Combine pin images with text
7. Write keyword-rich descriptions and boards
8. Add a link to descriptions
9. Upload videos
10. Include your website link on your post

Next, we will go through some important suggestions to improve your visibility on Pinterest.

Consistent Posting with Pins: One of the biggest suggestions with Pinterest is posting more often, as much as 10 times or more per day. It can improve engagement by up to 150%.

- Space your pins apart and avoid a burst of pinning. It expands the reach to more followers.
- Gather some people who will share and repost the pins.

Apply for Rich Pins: Rich pins are free Pinterest features. They allow for more detail and information, similar to Twitter Cards, or Facebook open graph. Below are 5 types of rich pins:

- Article pins: Include a headline, author name, story content and link
- Product pins: Include pricing, availability and where to purchase
- Recipe pins: Include recipe details
- Movie pins: Include reviews, ratings, and casting
- Place pins: Include how to find your company

More on Rich Pins: Rich pins are only for validated sites. You must apply for the ability to add rich pins from your website. The following list shows a step-by-step process:

- Add Pinterest HTML code to the blog
- Pinterest validation of the site
  - Request for rich pins – from validation tool
  - Get validation of rich pins – get a response the code was accepted

Another mistake many people make is posting the wrong sized pins. It turns off potential business and does not look professional. Numerous online websites can be used to create wonderful posts that are sized properly, like Canva, or Adobe Spark. Pinterest pins are best created for a vertical post.

For example:

A. 2:3 aspect ratio could be…
  - 600 pixels wide by 900 pixels height
  - 800 pixels wide by 1,200 pixels height
  - 1:3.5 aspect ratio could be…
  - 600 pixels wide by 2,100 pixels height
  - 400 pixels wide by 2,800 pixels height

Descriptions – Keyword rich and detailed. Think of these posting as an elevator pitch for a movie script, or query letter for a book. The average post must grab a user's attention in less than 3 seconds, which is why Facebook advises photos are the best form of advertisement. Below are some suggestions:

- Clear message
- Keywords
- Minimum wording – less is better (75 to 100 characters)
- Motivating sentiment
- Ask a question, give the reader something to do

Some steps promoted by Pinterest

- Use correct capitalization and punctuation
- No hashtags
- No promotional information ("10% off" or "Two for $9.99!")
- No salesy calls to action ("Buy now!")
- No references to Pinterest functionality ("Click here to pin!")

Extra descriptions are great; they provide an opportunity to educate on the product but save that for a pin close-up.

A few more suggestions to maximize engagement on Pinterest.

- Adding links give visitors a place to click for more information. Once you have captured someone's attention it's important to follow through with the engagement.
- Use multiple images when pinning posts.
- Combine images with text in posts (use overlapping text and headlines).

The last subject to discuss is "Pin it for Later." This option allows users to save something they can read later, which is great for bloggers.

When sharing a new post one special feature offers "Read it Later." This is a helpful tool that gives followers time to catch up later. Below are the directions:

- Pin an article and then add an image for the blog post
- Get the URL for the pin
- Share the URL along with the blog post, showing the user they can read it anytime.

Some final tips:

1. Categorize boards
2. Search for popular boards in your genre using "Find popular group boards" via PinGroupie and connect with the community
3. Observe Pinterest stats constantly. Adjust campaigns accordingly.
4. Avoid borders or alterations, like rounded corners.
5. Increase the brightness of pins for better visibility
6. Always add a company logo or brand name
7. Pinterest likes will help store future ideas
8. Follow boards that share your topics

9. Always verify URL links

10. Link your Pinterest account to Facebook and Twitter

11. Invite contributors to expand brand awareness

Chapter Seven:

Instagram or Snapchat

What is Snapchat?

Snapchat is an app that is designed for smartphones or tablets but has a distinctive quirk. The pictures or videos are only available for a short time, and then they disappear. The concept was designed to bring forth a more natural organic flow of engagement. Snapchat was initially intended to just focus on private, person-to-person photo sharing, but it is now available for a multitude of different tasks, like sending short videos, live video feeds, messaging and creating caricatures

What is Instagram?

Instagram is an app created for a smartphone or tablet designed for sharing photos and videos. The newsfeed runs like Twitter or Facebook and creates a profile account.

Many social media business users are wondering which is better, Instagram or Snapchat? So, we decided to give you the basics and let you decide. Below are 6 comparisons of the two platforms:

- Type of user
- Content style
- Discoverability
- Engagement stats
- Analytics
- Marketing ads

Both outlets have their purpose, and some businesses may thrive using the app while others might not see the same results. Before we start the explanation, here are some questions to consider:

1) What is your target audience using for an app?
2) What is the best content for your business, i.e. stories, images, videos?
3) What type of profile do you prefer, public or private?
4) Do you want to boost existing posts or run ads on the platform?

Instagram Users	Snapchat Users
400 million DU (Daily Use)	172M DU

More popular with women below age 49	More popular with users under 25 (60%)
Stories, images, videos	Stories and snaps
28% higher view rate	Views fall after posted on Instagram
Complete analytics	No native analytics/some paid analytics
Full ad management, powerful targeting tools	Full management, powerful target tools, but seemingly more expensive

In some cases, Instagram can be viewed as better than Snapchat by comparison. However, it's important to consider your audience. Judge the usage more by age in this case than anything else. Whereas Instagram is popular with the older generation, it still covers most everyone, while Snapchat is more effective with the younger crowd.

Why should you use Snapchat?

While users may not be familiar with Snapchat, it is one of the fastest-growing social networks out today. In 2015, it is estimated that there were 200 million active users on Snapchat, with 400 million snaps being sent per day.

Even if your target audience is not on Snapchat today, the chances are good that they will be soon.

Where Do I Start?

A Snapchat account can be set up in a few minutes. Below is a guide to get you started:

1) **Download the application and create an account:** It can be downloaded from Google Play or the App Store.

Once the app is downloaded, you will be asked to sign up for a new account. The username on Snapchat is very important. The username should align with your brand; it is the only way followers will recognize you. Snapchat does not have a profile like Twitter or Facebook; however, you can include a brief description of your company or business. The only identifier of your business is your username. Choose wisely!

The app will then ask you to enter your phone number to verify you are not a robot. Be sure to use a mobile phone number, as the app will send a text including a verification code. You can remove the phone number from your account later if you desire. However, if your business has a mobile phone number, it is a good idea to keep the number associated with your username. This way, when your customers use the "add friends from address book" feature, your Snapchat username will be listed, provided they have your business's number saved in their address book.

2) **Work with your settings:** The login screen will show a camera screen. Click on the ghost icon to adjust the settings. It is the user panel.

The last setting is whether users can send you snaps. In most cases, businesses use Snapchat for the story feature. The Snapchat story is a collection of pictures/videos created during 24 hours. These snaps can be viewed an unlimited number of times by your followers. The picture or video will disappear after 24 hours. In order to take advantage of this feature, be sure that your settings allow "everyone" to view your Snapchat story.

Some brands allow the user to send snaps, which is done to collect fan content or run contests. If you are planning to receive snaps from customers, make sure

that your settings allow all users to contact you
directly.

3) Send a snap: The camera screen has a
couple of options. The top-right icon is for
switching between front and rear cameras.
The icon on the left turns the flash on or off,
and to focus the camera you tap the screen.
Tap the large round button at the bottom to
take the picture. To take a video, tap and hold
the button, then release it when you want to
finish. Videos can be 10 seconds
When you are satisfied with the photo/video,
use the arrow at the bottom right corner and it
brings up a list of friends. To send a snap as
your story click on "My Story."

4) Add text, Emojis, drawings, and filters:
Emojis, doodle on your photo, and filters can
be added once your photo or video has been
taken.
Adding text or captions is allowed, up to
31characters. Captions automatically default
white in the opaque black bar. If you want
something bolder, tap the T again and create
large white text. Tap again to center the

caption. The text can be moved around by tapping and dragging or change the size by pinching the text in the way you would zoom in on a photo.

Emojis are added by tapping on the sticky note icon on the left text button. Changed your mind? Tap and drag the Emoji to the trash bin (which will appear in place of the sticky note once you begin to drag the Emoji). These fun features can also be modified in the same way text can.

If users want to draw something on their photo, use the pen tool on the top right. By tapping this feature, it allows you to choose a color by dragging your finger down the color picker. Once you have selected your color, begin to draw on your photo. If you make a mistake, use the undo button to the left of the pencil.

Snapchat offers three photo filters: sepia, saturated, and black and white. Real-time smart filters are also available on Snapchat. For example, you can add the current time or temperature to your photo/video.

Geofilters may also be available, depending on your location.

Use Instagram for promoting your business:

According to Statista, "Instagram is a mobile social network that allows users to edit and share photos as well as videos. In 2015, there were approximately more than 77.6 million active Instagram users in the United States. This figure is projected to surpass 111 million in 2019. Instagram is most popular with teens and young Millennials – this holds in the United States where more than half of Instagram's user base is between 18 and 29 years old."

A multitude of perceptive brands has joined the platform since its beginning in 2010. These retail brands have created stunning visual content, and clothing, media, and design-based brands are a natural fit. Instagram also has business-specific profiles. But why are brands rushing to join the social network?

Instagram is Easy to Use and Awesome!

The platform allows users to easily create stunning images. Twitter and Facebook optimize how photos are displayed and you can share them directly to Instagram (as well as to Tumblr, Foursquare, Flickr, and email) automatically or by individual selection.

Recently, Instagram introduced two new important features for visual storytelling: Instagram Stories and Instagram Live. Stories can be posted with either pics or video that are temporary viewable and self-delete in a designated time frame. It is similar to Snapchat. If using Live, it can be streamed from Instagram.

Below are 5 steps to improve this powerful tool:

1) **Images tell stories; they're not meant to blast your branding.** The product or service should be about the experience of doing business with your company. It is not a product placement ad. An example is Starbucks, where the focus is always on what the person is doing while drinking the coffee — on the beach, reading a book, etc. Obvious marketing will not positively increase brand awareness.

2) **Be strategic with your photos.** Make sure posts are created for a reason. Always keep them professional with good resolution, and sometimes

show a fun side of your company. Be deliberate about what and how you post.

3) Don't post too often. The general rule for posting is a couple of times a day. Any more than that is running the risk of manipulating the feed for personal gain. It will take time to figure out the best posting time and it depends on your audience.

Unfollowing is a common practice on Instagram, unlike Facebook or other platforms. PicFrame is an app that can be used to include several pics on one post. Just be sure the images are related to increasing the impact.

4) Account names are chosen as on Twitter. Handles are used for two purposes: To find users' profiles. If a user is tagged, it shows in a caption on the photo shared.

5) Use hashtags, but not every hashtag. Like on Twitter, hashtagging photos enables the discovery of your profile by users outside your primary connections. You can use the search functionality on the app to find out which hashtags are often used. Like on Twitter,

hashtagging Instagram photos by event, geolocation, or subject matter is a good idea.

People on Instagram tend to also use filters and colors as hashtags. Due to character length, hashtags are somewhat limited on Twitter. The freedom of no limits has encouraged Instagram users to get creative. This has inspired some users and brands to stuff Instagram captions with every hashtag imaginable. Avoid this temptation. It makes your brand look weak and worse; people may mistake it for spam.

If you have ever heard the adage "a picture is worth 1,000 words" it is still true, although the rules have changed slightly. Now, it's 10,000 likes.

Chapter Eight:

Using LinkedIn?

What's Does Your Profile Say About You??

LinkedIn is considered the best option for the professional crowd. It is based more on networking resources, hiring, and finding job placement, gathering sales leads, and real-time industry news. But a word of caution: the platform is less user-friendly. It may even seem daunting; however, we are here to help you over that hurdle. Below are some steps for maximizing your profile:

1) **Complete your profile page:** Include all important details. Remember, an incomplete profile does not look professional.

2) **Emphasize your expertise:** Set up an image of professionalism, it puts you in the expert category.

3) **Create a call to action:** Write a precise call to action directive to explain your profession, something like see my website for further

information. Make it clear and detailed; no one can read your mind.

4) **Always, always include a professional photo:** You can go to a local photographer and have high-quality pics done for a minimal charge. Selfies are not a preferred method.

5) **Optimize profile searches:** There are millions of people searching on LinkedIn, so your profile should be easily found. Do some research on the best keywords to give you the best chance of expanding a brand.

6) **Consistent posting:** Not only does posting help engagement, but it also improves organic SEO optimization.

7) **Create and actively participate in groups:** Networking is still one of the best marketing tools. Choose 2 or 3 of the biggest topics within your genre and discuss the topics with others.

8) **Be conscious about your connections:** LinkedIn is a professional platform; it's not Facebook. Some people will examine your profile for people with whom you associate. Spammers are a real issue on social media.

9) **Personalize messages:** Enable followers to connect with your message or brand.

10) **Learn/understand and follow trending content tools:** LinkedIn offers a tool to show content trends and allows you to weed out unwanted information.

Build Your Network

Once the specifics of setting up your profile are complete, it is time to start building a network. However, LinkedIn connections are vastly different than other platforms. The basis was designed for the professional networker. Therefore, be mindful of who you are accepting into your connection list.

Best options for connecting: Sending invitations on LinkedIn must be done with a high degree of professionalism. The clientele basis was founded for the businessman or woman. When creating a request take the time to explain your brand and why you are interested in connecting with that person.

Join the conversation: Many users get stuck once they build their network because they fail to join in on conversations. When building your brand, show off your knowledge, engage with other posts that pertain to your expertise.

What to share: The way someone presents themselves is very important. Start with sharing some newsworthy articles that relate to your area of expertise. If you have a blog or content that is produced by your company, use it to create a post that people can engage with. According to Constant Contact, "sharing it on your profile will help get it in front of people that have a vested interest in your industry and will be more likely to comment or share. Even better – use LinkedIn's Publisher feature to share your blog post. Publisher will give that article visibility in the feeds of your followers and will add it to your profile as an article" (Pinkham, 2019).

Unadvisable posts: As stated above, LinkedIn is a business professional social platform, so uploading pictures of your kids, funny jokes, reality TV news, sports rants, political rants, complaints about your boss, what you had for breakfast, what you want for lunch, your favorite type of ice cream … Can you see where this is leading? Create a personal website on another platform to share stuff that pertains to your private life, but if your business is titled with a real name, for example, Lizzy McNett, then you must be cautious of everything that is posted. A quick Google search can tell a completely different story.

Explore the platform: LinkedIn has a multitude of outlets to share your brand with the community, such as the Work Tab.

LinkedIn Groups: These are sections that connect like-minded peers centered around a single topic.

Additional options:

- Slideshare houses presentations
- Infographics
- Documents, and more

Users can search for information on industry topics, bookmark slides they want to save in a clipboard, and upload their presentations to share with their peers.

Seven Qualities to Assist in Creating Authority on LinkedIn

Admittedly, LinkedIn may not be the most entertaining platform on the social media market; nonetheless, it is the most useful for expanding your business. At first glance, LinkedIn can be intimidating, but with some planning and practice, it will become a valuable tool for expanding your brand.

1) Who has viewed your profile: A great feature provided by LinkedIn to analyze is the profile? It provides insight into people who have viewed your profile for the last 90 days. The tool can be used to optimize your profile for the right audience.

The tool allows users to look at the name, headline, location, industry, and how the people found you. Plus, users can view what keywords they were using, their title, and more. Stats can provide awareness of how your profile is perceived by the public.

2) Your profile: One of the most important tools of any platform is the profile section. The important areas to make you stand out are linking to visual examples of your work in your LinkedIn profile summary and job experience sections. Once that is completed, add documents, photos, links, videos, or presentations.

3) Your headline: Under your name is a great place to introduce yourself to followers or

protentional clients. Write a compelling headline to grab attention.

4) **Connections' activity:** This tool is a great advantage for anyone looking to get an insight into their connections, or gain some ideas to give their profile a facelift. Plus, great conversations can be started by gaining a better sense of people's personalities, interests, needs, and concerns.

5) **Groups:** This area can open the door to meet new people, ideas, and gain resources for your business. They offer a platform to discuss industry trends and news, post job openings, ask for opinions, and share expertise.

6) **Publisher:** This tool is an excellent way to connect with followers in a long-form format, outside of the limited post on your regular feed. Publisher allows users to get a more in-depth look at your professional thoughts. The section is searchable on or off LinkedIn. Plus, Publisher offers the

ability to manage comments, edit and delete posts, view stats, and tag.

7) **LinkedIn app:** There's not much else to say in this section, except that you can get the app from Google Play or iTunes.

Writer's Publishing House

We provide exclusive features along with the following guidelines:

- Social Media Marketing
- Cost-Effective Marketing Resources

Online marketing is the action of advertising and marketing the products or services of a business over the internet. Advertising relies upon websites or emails to reach the intended users, combined with e-commerce to facilitate business transactions.

Social Media Development & Training - We will manage your social media marketing or train your marketing staff. Do you need a social media strategy or social media calendar we got you covered?

Email Marketing (Constant Contact Certified) - Do you have an Email Marketing system in place? We can help you set up and activate your Constant Contact 60-day free trial.

Local SEO and Reputation Marketing- Writer's Publishing House Social Media Marketing helps manage the public facts about your brand across the popular local directories' consumers search online.

Drive more search traffic to your business. Local SEO increases web traffic, leads, and sales from local visitors – If you're a local company, getting web visits and leads from users in a different city, state, or country won't do anything to build your business. With local SEO, you increase traffic from consumers in your specific service areas, which means you'll get a higher visit-to-sale rate.

Outsource Marketing- Our Services include Marketing Strategy, Content Strategy, Branding & Graphic Design, Collateral Development, Video Development, Digital Media, Ghost Writing, Translation, Website Design, Strategic Communications, and Remote Staffing.
Content Strategy- We can create your business social media toolkits, Social Media Calendars, and develop all your content for all your social media sites
Strategic Communications- Let us promote your brand through events, promotions, social media ads, press releases.

Branding & Graphic Design- We have a team of Creative Designers that develop anything that you can imagine.

Learn more at ww.writerspublishinghouse.com

Chapter Nine:

SEO Optimization: It's all about the algorithms

Search Engine Optimization (SEO) is the process of improving a website or app's presence in organic (free) search results. SEO differs from paid search campaigns where a marketer must pay for placement in search results.

What is an SEO Audit?

An SEO audit is a review of a website, with the intent of improving the site's rankings in organic search results. The assessments are performed with specialized tools, or by an experienced SEO consultant.

Why Audit a website or App?

There are several reasons to consider an audit, but the most common are:

a) Organic traffic has declined

b) A redesign of a website or app

c) Site migration

d) Consolidation

e) Rebrand

f) Or other major technical, content, link-related events

Technical debate (refactoring is not only a result of poorly written code but is also done based on an evolving understanding of a problem, and the best way to solve that problem) has been built upon your website. Several items can cause this issue to escalate; for example, plugins or other technology can interfere with functionality, or worse yet, get in the way of search engine bots, browsers, and users.

Website content must stay updated to keep your site ranking high in search engine results, along with eliminating outdated keywords.

- If the website contains content duplication it may cause an over indexation or eroding of page authority. The issue lowers search engine results.

- Any blocked or hidden content could cause indexation concerns. Users will be restricted from finding your website if search engines cannot find all the present content.

- If your website has slower load times, visitors find the issue frustrating and it signals search engines to assign a lower rank. It will lower organic SEO results and conversion rates.

- A website that is not secure (https) could risk your visitors' privacy and can trigger warnings in their browser. It is becoming increasingly important to have a more secure site. The same concept applies to sites that are non-transactional, especially if competitors have https security protocols.

- Poor mobile sites can lead to unsatisfied visitors, climbing bounce rate, and decreased keyword rankings based on Google's understanding of low user satisfaction.

- Broken links (links from your website to other websites), inbound links (links from other websites to yours), or internal links (links from one page of your site to another) may lower your site's trust and authority.

- Google Webmaster Guidelines not being followed may lead to the devaluation of the site, making it less visible to users.

SEO Audits

The best practices for an audit are once or twice a year; however, it can vary depending on the industry or content strategy. Some examples:

- Website content changes regularly
- Code changes frequently on your website
- Multiple individuals contribute to your site
- Your industry changes quickly online
- Your industry is highly competitive online

The best way to think of having an SEO audit is by getting an annual physical with your doctor, or a wellness exam. Results show potential problems on the existing site, solutions to solve the issues, along with recommendations to increase performance.

Benefits of an SEO Audit

- Identify technical problems to resolve site performance in search engine results, thereby improving organic searches.
- Identify content opportunities
- Digital health analytics
- Current backlink profile
- Improve the overall use of the website for users and search engines

- Elevate rankings related to keyword searches, increase conversations through leads and online sales.
- Establish a passive income through marketing channels
- Learn how search engines are viewing the website

What SEO Audits Include

Performance audits can include the following depending on your situation:

- Domains
- Subdomains
- URLs
- Redirects
- 404 page
- Robots.txt
- Indexing issues
- Crawl issues
- Canonicalization issues
- Page load time
- Structured data recommendations
- HTML and XML sitemaps
- Navigation and file structure

- Template-specific recommendations
- Internal linking strategies
- External linking strategies
- Keywords
- Page titles and meta tags
- Content
- Duplicate content
- Thin pages
- Under-optimized pages
- Data feed optimization
- Conversions
- Analytics
- Webmaster accounts
- Local targeting
- Citation improvements
- Image optimization
- Mobile optimization
- International targeting
- Google News inclusion
- Digital assets
- Social media indicators
- Blog optimization
- Information architecture

- Usability concerns
- Coordination with ADA requirements
- Knowledge graph optimization

How are SEO Audits Received?

Once the initial audit is completed, the analytics will be evaluated by one of our experts and then a meeting will be planned to review the results. A strategy can be created to solve the issues.

Free SEO Audit Tools

- **Google Search Console** is consulted before any actions. The domains must be accepted.
- **Google Analytics** – Analytics are crucial to the SEO audit process. Data provides the ability to track Key Performance Indicators (KPIs) and measure the impact of the recommendations for the audit results. The data provided in Google Analytics allows us to track specific KPIs and measure the impact of the recommendations contained in the SEO audit deliverables.
- **Bing Webmaster Tools** – Bing Webmaster Tools provide insights that are not contained in any of the Google tools.

- **Chrome Developer Tools** – These tools allow the user to see how crawlers and browsers interact with your site. The page speed is crucial to any SEO audit. Chrome Developer Tools reveal which page elements are slowing users down.

Paid SEO Audit Tools

The paid tools for an SEO audit are almost endless, but below are a few of the favorites.

- MOZ – Keyword Research
- STAT – Keyword Rank Tracking
- PitchBox – Outreach Prospecting, Campaign Management, and Reporting
- Spyfu – Keyword Research and Competitive Analysis
- ahrefs – Backlink Analysis, Outreach Prospecting, and Competitive Analysis
- Content King – Content Performance Tracking and Monitoring
- Crawlers
- Screaming Frog – Website Crawling and Searching and Extracting Code

- Deep Crawl – Web-based Crawling of Large Websites

Arguments for and Against SEO Audit Tools

SEO audit tools can eat up a budget with little to no results, or the user finds the analytics vague and complicated, so it's important to understand your current needs. Granted, the tools give wonderful tracking performance if you don't have a robust team to sort through the particulars; however, the cost may be a wasteful resource. The best results come from a well-planned strategy, and that comes from individuals. In some cases, the financial expense may bring forth unexpected results in the end.

International SEO Marketing

Glossary definitions: "hreflang tags are a technical solution for sites that have similar content in multiple languages. The owner of a multilingual site wants search engines to send people to the content in their language. Say a user is Dutch and the page that ranks is English, but there's also a Dutch version."

Domain names for international SEO. You may want to consider a few things when choosing a domain name for your international SEO campaigns. Some domains, known as country code top-level domains (ccTLD), will default to a specific location.

Website Expansion

The aspects of international SEO are wildly misunderstood. The intricacies are more than HREFLANG, ccTLDs (country-targeted top-level domains), and geo-targeting. It's imperative to map the expansion campaign and understand the market in the areas you want to expand into.

If you have decided to increase your brand internationally, there are several items to learn before changing the site settings. Items of interest:

- The countries into which you're expanding
- Those countries' main languages, and
- How your business offerings might change in the new markets

Writer's Publishing House Social Media Marketing has the tools to offer such expansion in the event your company wants to grow your brand internationally.

Languages

Business offerings across the web must incorporate different languages, to accommodate translating content so search engines can guide users to the best options.

Action Items:

- Translations are best done manually; it is the best option for branding issues and user preferences.
- Put your HREFLANG in XML sitemaps. However, this is not your only option, except that it keeps code off your page. This will increase page speed.
- Don't use a ccTLD. It is for Geo-targeting only.

Keep in Mind:

It is not necessary to change the ccTLDs or geotargeting; producing good translations and using the correct site markup will get the desired results.

SEO Marketing for Local Branding

In many businesses, there is one common struggle that is difficult to avoid: competitors. The goal must be to gain traction over other local retailers. Although, going against the larger companies with auto-generated local listings is challenging. Plus, years of playing the SEO game increases the difficulty.

One of the most demanding obstacles for many local businesses is how to stay up to date with Google's ever-evolving list of ranking factors; updates like the "Possum" can disrupt any strategy. The algorithm changes allowed businesses outside city limits to compete for local spots if they service that area.

Ten SEO Tips to Help Move the Needle for Local Market Branding

Claim Your Business Listings

Once you have claimed your business listing, it is time to claim any duplicate listings that develop over time. The listings can be claimed and then any duplicates can be removed. Finding the listings can seem daunting, but there are tools to assist in this process. Moz Local is one great option to locate all local listings.

The process is easy: First, enter the business name and zip code. Be specific on the business spelling, capitalizations, abbreviations, etc. Select your business from the results and Moz will serve you the complete, incomplete, inconsistent, and duplicate listings tied to your business.

Add Location Pages to Your Website

To get the best results when search engines crawl your site for the best possible matches, it is important to have a specific landing page for each of your business locations. The address should include suite numbers and the exact physical location.

Improve NAP Consistency

What is NAP?

"The acronym NAP stands for Name, Address, Phone number, and it's critical for any business that wants to rank well in local organic search results" (Corona, 2018).

Search engines need to have accurate information on the business name, address, and phone number (NAP), and this information must be consistent everywhere.

The information must be specific, not just your name and address. For example, if the title includes LLC, Co., or Inc., add the acronyms. Be consistent with the information listed on the website.

The Moz local search tool allows much of the information to be updated. Start with the Google Business Listing.

Update Everything on my Google My Business

Accurate information is imperative for everyday traffic across the Internet, particularly for optimized SEO search engine results.

Log into your Google My Business (GMB) account and update any outdated information. It is very important to fill in as much information as possible. Be thorough.

The listing should be appealing:

- Logo
- Avatar/profile pic
- Interior photos
- Exterior photos
- Product photos

All images should be high-quality resolutions. You only get one chance at a first impression. Update the info for all business locations.

Attain Reviews

One of the most important factors in allowing your business to grow is reviews. People want to read what others have thought of your services, products, or customer service. Good reviews pack a powerful punch; however, the reviews must be legitimate, so do not fake them. If customers receive quality service, writing a review will not be a problem.

The reviews not only help your business ranking, but they also increase search results. By expanding real estate on a web search, SEO results will improve. As your demand increases, so will your Google ranking.

Peer ranking is a highly social advantage. When users see a 5-star review it tackles three major components at one time:

- Ranking
- Click-through rate (CTR)
- Conversion rate optimization (CRO)

Create Local Content

When you create content in the business niche it will make an impact on the local search ranking.

Google AdWords Keyword Planner

AdWords Keyword Planner is a great FREE tool when it comes to establishing your local SEO keywords. The research will offer keywords that have the highest search volume along with the lowest. Plus, it helps you find similar terms for local audiences.

Backlinks from Partners and Sponsorships

Create a list of businesses and organizations that you partner with or sponsor, and then contact them and ask that they add a link to their website. Make sure you reciprocate the offer.

Local Link Building

Gaining backlinks from high domain authority websites will highly impact your local presence. This is one area that cannot be stressed enough.

Utilize Social Media Platforms

Do not underestimate the usage of social media platforms. They are a powerful financial asset at your fingertips. Plus, it's free marketing. Google will crawl and pull search results from social platforms, such as Facebook profiles and reviews, your business's

LinkedIn or YouTube, and even Twitter accounts and recent tweets.

In the next section are some suggestions on optimizing for local SEO growth. According to SEO Expert, "The ways of how we search using search engines and the content delivered to us are always changing. But one thing for sure is that search engines are clearly on a mission to provide users with the most relevant results for their query, personalized based on their location, search history, and browsing behavior" (Shaw, 2019).

The following is a checklist you can follow to optimize to grow a local business:

- Boost SEO by adding keywords to any website
- Include business contact information such as name, address, and phone number (NAP).
- Always encourage customers to leave quality reviews. If you need to remove a Facebook review, read this.
- Be prompt when responding to reviews, even if it is negative. You will not be able to please everyone all the time, but use the knowledge to better your customer service.

- Upload at least ten quality photographs so users will recognize your business quickly.
- Stay active. Keep business profiles updated with the latest news.

Chapter Ten:

Reputation Management

What is Reputation Management?

It is one of the most important factors of owning or operating a business. Negative reviews or reputations can be difficult to overcome unless the situation is handled correctly. Negative events that can impact reputation in a single instant may include scandals, criminal acts, product recalls, bad press, lawsuits, negative reviews, etc.

Online Reputation Management (ORM)

Since the development of the Internet, companies have emerged all over to manage reputation issues. Search results like Google, social media sites, Yelp, and beyond can surface after a negative incident.

Five Ways to Get Started with Reputation Marketing

1) **Audit content:** One of the first steps to controlling online reputation is actively participating in content inventories. Address all concerns about the online content before releasing it to any public

site. Head off all feedback from followers or editorials about you or your business.

2) Track conversations: The adage "You only get one shot at a first impression" rings true. Once the public experiences an organization, business, company, or person, a reputation is formed. It can be good, bad, or anything in between.

Track all conversations to measure quality sentiment. Then, learn areas of opportunity to improve your brand. Always maintain control of the content, conversation, and communication among stakeholders.

3) Install reputation marketers: Every business need management, especially in the area of reputation. It is best to either hire someone or maintain a high level of scrutiny over the content being released. The action will help control the company's mission statement.

4) Coaching consistency: Any successful business runs on consistency; it is a necessary evil to ensure a quality reputation among the public. Anyone involved, no matter how small a part they

play, should know and understand their role in your mission brand.

5) **Empowering surprise:** One unexpected marketing advantage is the element of surprise. It can be categorized as the moment when a customer is amazed by your company and becomes ready to spread the good word. However, surprise cannot be a normal event. Instead, use the quality of work produced to motivate customers to enhance your brand organically.

Videos

Video marketing has been on a steady rise for years. In fact, according to Forrester Research, videos show 50% more organic first page searches than traditional text pages. I'd say that is an impressive beginning!

One main reason for creating online marketing videos is they are an attractive way to connect with potential clients. Plus, video production is relatively inexpensive. Once the recording is finished, it can stay online forever. In other words, the benefits outweigh the cost of marketing over time.

In addition to the online benefits, video marketing and social media go hand in hand since most social media platforms encourage posting and sharing to promote engagement. The opportunities to have a video go viral are limitless. Let's get recording!

If this is your first time creating a video, we have some suggestions to help make it a success:

1) **Title:** Like with any marketing plan, the title is highly important. It is what will bring impressions and encourage people to share and repost. Don't forget the appropriate keywords in your title. They will help online search engines to locate your channel, website, or social media profile.

2) **Content:** It's important to write good content. The same applies to any marketing venue: content, content, and better content. Tip: Keep all videos short until you have a faithful following. At that point, you can study analytics.

3) **A good length is between 3 to 5 mins. URL:** One way to engage the audience is to use the add text box to your video. It's a great tool for

adding a website address, tips, special messages, sales, or requests.

4) **Branding Images:** During the video, it's important to display your business logo. You can keep it as a permanent image or flash it several times during the process. The best possible place to display the brand is the upper left-hand corner.

5) **HTML Link:** A common mistake is leaving out the hyperlink to direct traffic. If viewers like your information, they will want to locate you easily. One way to deter traffic is by not making yourself available to be contacted by potential clients.

6) **Video Reach:** Many marketers limit themselves to YouTube, however, video marketing goes beyond the average video channels. Websites are the best way to connect with internet traffic, so why not captivate them on your website or app?

Finally, Google algorithms factor impressions into any organic search results. Embedded video views receive a much higher rating for search analytics.

Reasons Any Company Needs Video Marketing

Wonder why you should be using video marketing? Honestly stated, "YouTube is the 2nd largest search engine on the web and by 2020, 75% of mobile traffic will be video," according to Cisco (Buffa, 2013).

In other words, if your business does not yet video market, it is time to start. Video marketing provides the following advantages:

1) **Increases engagement:** Statistics prove time again that visual content is key to user engagement. One of the main reasons is the ease of shareability across social media. Think back to the reason social media was created: to socialize. What better way to engage with an audience than a video? "Audiences are about 10 times more likely to engage, share, and comment on video content compared to blogs or related social posts. In fact, videos on Facebook business pages increase end-user engagement by 33%. Take our Starbucks

Unicorn Frapp video as an example! This was a fun video our team made together trying out current trends and got 1.4k views on Facebook" (Readyartwork, n.d.).

2) **Add personality to your brand:**

Yes, pictures are said to be worth a thousand words, but videos can bring millions to your brand.

According to readyartwork, "Videos are perfect for company branding and increase brand awareness by 52%." This alone is a very good reason to start a video marketing strategy.

3) **Showcase your products or services**: One question, why use a flat image when you can create a 3D realm to cabinet and display the usage of a product? For example, why display a pair of shoes when you can highlight the color and see the product in use?

4) **Provide visual explanations:** "The human brain prefers visuals, in fact, 90% of information transmitted to the brain is visual and people retain 80% of what they see in

comparison to only 20% of what they read! So, don't make it difficult for your customers. Instead make it visual, like this informative conservation video we made for the City of Monrovia. A large amount of text would be so exhausting to read, but as a video, the information is more easily retained and understood" (readyartwork, n.d.).

5) **Show your company's accomplishments:** It is important to showcase achievements and capabilities to current followers or potential clients. Videos are a perfect way to capture users' attention.

6) **Elevate retention rates on your website:** "If the content is in a video, 65% of viewers watch more than ¾ of a video, which is more than most text-based content. Videos on retail sites keep visitors an average of 2 minutes longer so your company can capitalize on this by utilizing a video loop on your website" (readyartwork, n.d.).

A video is the first and last thing visitors see on your website, so why not entice them to stay longer and review all the services offered?

7) **Increase conversion rates and boost sales:** The main reason to use video marketing is to improve customer sales. "Studies also show that 85% of customers are more likely to make a purchase after watching a product video" (readyartwork, n.d.).

Podcasts

Ever since our ancestors started drawing or carving on cave walls, the importance of storytelling has played a crucial role in the advancement of society. The ancient scrolls of humans are revered; a cherished heritage that we can learn about the past. And this is a concept that continues to radiate among current generations.

Video has somewhat diminished the allure of using podcasts in some areas of entertainment, but they have flourished in many avenues since the invention of smart mobile technology. Podcasts can be created to directly communicate with the listener. It is a more intimate way of passing the information along to the subscriber.

A valuable asset of podcasts is they are an easy, convenient way to communicate. They can be downloaded on any digital device and taken anywhere, unlike videos that require more memory and connection to watch.

Creating podcasts can deliver a digital marketing outlet that reduces the costs associated with postage, printing, or paper generated products. Plus, they are compatible with email restrictions on file size.

Because podcasts are delivered digitally, they eliminate many costs associated with other forms of communication. They can also reduce meeting costs and e-mail storage costs. They are easy to archive and updating them is quick and easy.

In society, time efficiency is highly important to many business owners, and using podcasts for clients is an effective use of their time. It's something they can consume while meeting the daily demands of life. By saving time, you can improve productivity.

One last suggestion: Podcasts are a great way to develop your social networking strategy. Over time, subscribers are essential to deepening the effectiveness of your brand.

Why Blog, Blog, and More Blogging?

The benefits of blogging are limitless for any business. If you think for a moment about how many times you were unsure of how something is done, the first thing you did was Google search the topic. What happens? You get results on the subject matter. At that point, you can determine the best site to find answers. The majority of listings are blogs of some kind. Blogging has become the new age of encyclopedias. Below are the advantages of blogging:

1. Drives website traffic
2. Helps turn traffic into leads
3. Creates the authority status of the author
4. Brings forth long-term results
5. Provides opportunities for guest blogging

Blog posts provide consistent traffic each day. Many of these potential leads will come from blog articles, although it's important to incorporate all the marketing tools we have discussed in the various sections of this book.

One additional option for blogging is to test large campaigns at minimal costs. By building an audience for the new product or whatever the campaign may be, you can save money using property that's already owned. Instead of investing in advertising with someone else, get some response from current followers. After the results are analyzed it will be easier to make any necessary adjustments before publishing a big campaign.

Any company or small business can benefit from a blog. It has also become popular with individuals who want to tell their stories or educate the public on certain topics. Happy blogging!

The Best Blogging Tools & Resources

- Mindmeister
- Evernote
- Trello
- Google Calendar
- Focus Booster
- Unroll.me
- Sidekick.com
- Dropbox.com

- Statscount
- Screenflow
- Pdf Escape
- Grammerly.com
- Blogger.com
- Transcribe
- Google alerts.com
- Wisestamp
- shareaholic.com
- Triberr:
- Scoop.it
- Pocket

Webinars

One of the best marketing solutions is using a cross-platform. Since the invention of the Internet, the medium of marketing outlets has expanded dramatically. One such option is offering webinars for current clients or potential clients. It is a highly effective way to sell products and services.

Webinar marketing is one way to connect with a broader audience and promote your business. Most webinar tools provide free lead generation options and offer essential information on improving ROI at the end of the webinar.

A normal webinar presentation consists of the presenter's program, followed by a Q&A session. Due to the visual medium, it is much easier to connect with participants since most people are visual learners. Some webinar presentation ideas include:

- Expound on products or services or sometimes both
- Educate on published content or blog postings
- Lecture on a particular service

One word of caution: Webinars are not a sales pitch. You must provide the participants with a valuable service to improve their life. By educating them on your product or service, it grants them the opportunity to make a purchase.

According to MakeSocialMediaSell, webinars retain 40% of the viewers' attention. Up to that 40% who attend will become qualified leads. The additional percentage will buy something from your services. However, only half of the registered individuals will attend the webinar. But the results seen by other companies endeavor a worthwhile risk.

There is one key point that any marketing tool must include: Make sure you offer a solution to ease the participant's pain. Then provide options for solving the issues with outlets. Always let the customer decide the best choice that suits their needs.

The ideal period is 60 minutes, shutting down in 45 minutes and opening the floor to questions. Or, another option would be to take a ten-minute break after 30 minutes for communication with participants, then end with another option for additional questions. It's critical to be highly organized and prepared. You are the expert! Below are some webinar hosting services:

- GotoWebinar
- Cisco WebEx
- ClickMeeting
- Anymeeting
- Instant Teleseminar
- Zoom
- WebinarJam
- EasyWebinar

If you are concerned about financial restraints, YouTube Live is a free option and wildly popular. The video can be made available on Wistia or Vimeo.

Chapter Eleven:

Running Ads

In literal terms, advertising is the process of making your business merchandise or services known to an audience. It is generally done through some type of media outlet. It's a creative positioning in the media, in a timely fashion, used in a specific strategic way.

The best uses of advertising money involve designing a campaign that aligns with the wants and needs of your client's genre. The key is to generate excitement for a product or service. These questions are very important when designing an advertising campaign:

- Why should someone do business with your company?
- What will they get from your product or services?
- Who are you?

There are some major differences between marketing and advertising that you should be aware of and understand. Firstly, marketing is the concept of preparing a product for the market place. Secondly, advertising is the act of placing the product before an audience. If you find the difference between the two confusing, you are not alone.

Advertising is only one segment of the marketing process. The ability to run an ad is done by purchasing the ad space. It's an announcement that is created by an identifiable sponsor, brand, or business logo to persuade an audience to buy the product. The advertisement placement can be anywhere, like magazines, direct mail, email, websites, blogs, TV, radio, or public transit.

Marketing, on the other hand, is the methodical preparation and application of controlling the mix between intended buyers and sellers for the beneficial exchange of products and services. Marketing is a step-by-step process that starts with selling your merchandise – a short compelling description to explain your business. Think of marketing as one piece of the pie. The rest includes advertising, market research, media planning, community relations, and sales strategy. Intermingled with all this is customer service, a huge portion of any successful business. The preparation of any advertising campaign is critical to its success.

Reasons to Consider Paid Social Media Advertising

According to The State of Tech, "92% of small businesses will increase their investment in social media this year." (Heing, 2018).

If you are still wondering why you should pay for social media advertising, keep reading. Statistics prove that more than two billion users are on social media each day. It breaks down to 135 minutes in 24 hours. Plus, the number of small businesses advertising on Facebook has doubled to fifty million recently.

One tip: Paid social media advertising is quite different than traditional outbound marketing. Since the initiation of Big Data, the ability to pinpoint exact target audiences is simple. Social media platforms are designed to facilitate the achievement of business goals such as lead generation, website traffic, brand awareness, and much more. Ad programs also grant access to native analytics to help improve campaign success.

Below are seven advantages of using paid social media advertising:

- Amplify your reach
- Fit any budget
- Enhance your targeting
- Boost brand awareness
- Maximize your content marketing
- Gain access to mobile users
- Gather market insights

1) **Amplify Reach:** Marketing helps to promote brand visibility. Facebook algorithms now give priority to friends and family over organic searches. Since the sheer volume of posts has increased exponentially, the statistical chance of people seeing your posts has declined significantly. In the case of paid ads campaigns, they are guaranteed to be placed on a user's feed. Despite the noise of the larger social platform, this gives you a direct window to drive leads, website traffic, and sales. Success will come when you find where your audience spends their time online.

2) **Fit Any Budget:** Paid marketing is a highly cost-effective way to promote businesses. The ads are run on a pay-per-click (PPC) schedule. This means you pay when someone clicks on the link, plus you get the benefit of impressions. In other words, free advertising. One advantage is the ability to advertise with your niche markets at a discount. Once a few ad cycles have run, you can refine the targeting to drive better ROI.

3) **Enhance Targeting:** Paid advertising lets the user have complete control over the ad and their audience. All the platforms allow for a plethora of targeting parameters. Factors include interests, hobbies, personality types, and more. By uploading a list of contacts to target, or creating a similar audience, it gives a powerful base for expanding to an ideal audience.

Another option is the ability to retarget users that have already visited your website. Simply install the Facebook retargeting pixel on your site and previous visitors will see ads for your company in their News Feed.

4) **Boost Brand Awareness:** The social media campaign is the most cost-effective way to expand your brand reach. When your business appears in the regular News Feed users will recognize and begin to engage with posts.

> "Consider that 80% of its users follow at least one brand on Instagram. Of this majority group, at least 30% of users have purchased a product they discovered on Instagram" (Heing, 2018).

5) **Maximize Content Marketing:** Social media is one of the best ways to circulate brand awareness.

> "According to Sprout Social, 73.4% of users follow a brand because they're interested in its product or service. Nurture the curiosity of your followers with educational content that will transform them into qualified leads" (Heing, 2018).

This will not only increase social media traffic, but it will also drive website traffic, boost engagement on social media, and improve the ROI of your content marketing.

6) **Access Mobile Users Anytime:** The penetration of social media advertising is unparalleled. "According to Pew Research, 80% of the time spent on social media is spent on a mobile device" (Heing, 2018).

   When businesses pay for social media advertising, users will see the ads and learn about how to purchase the products. The most effective ads emulate the organic content of their native platform.

7) **Gather Market Insights:** Several questions can be answered with social media, such as:

   1. How did your audience interact with your ads?
   2. Which ad type was most popular?
   3. Did video convert better – and with whom?

The use of native analytics on social media platforms helps to assess and refine the performance of advertising campaigns. Look to KPIs such as clicks, comments, and profile visits to determine if your ads are creating an impact. Facebook Insights is the gold standard of platform analytics.

All the social media platforms indeed have their brand of advertising, however, that does not mean business owners should use each one of them. The first step is to study which one perform organically the best. In other words, find the best possible fit for your product or services. For example, look at the audience: According to Hootsuite, Pinterest has more female users than males, and if you want a younger crowd Snapchat or Instagram is best.

Once you have decided which outlet is the best option for your business it's time to look at the types of ads that are available.

Facebook Ads

Facebook designed its ads to help achieve one of three types of campaign intentions:

- Awareness
- Consideration
- Conversion

Awareness: This is the act of building an audience that knows or follows your company. Branding is the essence of running a successful business.

Consideration: Using the consideration objective will drive traffic to your website, increase engagement, encourage app installs, or improve video views. Plus, the ad can generate leads and encourage communication.

Conversion: The basic use of conversions is to improve online conversations and drive traffic to an offline store.

Facebook is a popular demographic that has the potential for driving enormous brand awareness if used in the right fashion.

Several Formats Are Available:

Photo Ads

When you run a Facebook ad it includes a photo and 125 characters of text. The text incorporates the title and link description, plus call-to-action buttons. The option also applies to posts that can be promoted, or use Facebook Business Manager.

Tip: Facebook ads are great when showcasing new products or services. It allows the business owner to promote a product rather than just posting a photo of the product or service.

Video Ads

Another great option Facebook offers is 30 to 60-second promotion video ads. However, as with any other ads, choosing the right audience is critical. Create solid goals, and market the right audience to get the best results.

Video ads can also work well with a TV ad campaign. The TV part of the ad does not have to align with the same content, because it is a great way to draw in an audience. It can be used to highlight the best part of your brand.

Tip: The best results will come from videos that are 15 seconds or less.

Carousel Ads

A unique adoption is carousel advertising. They allow business owners to create ads with up to 10 images or videos. Each one includes an individual link. One particular option with this type of marketing is having the ability to showcase different features of a product or service or explain a process for multiple products.

Tip: When creating an ad, it must provide a story. Lead the follower in, tell the story, and solve their problem.

Slideshow Ads

These types of ads create a video using static images. It offers compelling motion, yet requires no video resources. It's a great alternative to video ads.

Tip: Slideshow ads load quickly, even on slower connection speeds.

Collection Ads

These ads are a great way to show products right in the Facebook feed. They include a cover photo or video. You can add product images with pricing along with other details. Users can learn more about your business.

Tip: These are perfect for travel agencies or other destination offers.

Messenger Ads

Messenger ads are placed on the home screen of the messenger app. The best use is to encourage people to connect with your business or link to your website.

Lead Ads

Lead ads are only on mobile devices and include pre-populated contact forms. They are a great way to build an email database or get users to sign up for a newsletter, request a free trial, or quote. The leads can create a good sales funnel.

Tip: For the best results, collect the most information upfront as possible.

Instagram Ads

If you are not aware, Facebook owns Instagram, so support can be found via the Facebook Business Manager. All ads support the same three categories:

- Awareness
- Consideration
- Conversation

Audience

Instagram has its audience separate from Facebook, so don't confuse the two and think the ad should be the same. Millennials migrate to this platform, but plenty of Generation X users also like the social media site. Instagram also emulates Facebook ads with photos, videos, and a carousel.

Photo and Video Ads

Instagram photo or video ads will look similar to normal posts, except they have a sponsored image on the top right. Campaign options may let you use a call-to-action button.

Tip: All ads should resemble regular posts and messages. It is important to stay with your brand identity.

Carousel Ads

Instagram carousel ads have arrows to swipe or scroll the images.

Instagram Story Ads

The ad includes up to 15-second-long videos or images. They appear in full-display format between other stories.

Tip: The ads only last for 24 hours, so make the content relevant or limited offers from your business.

Twitter Ads

Twitter ads have six business objectives:

- **Website clicks or conversions:** Promote Tweets to people who you want to visit and act on your website. You're charged per click.

- **Tweet engagement:** Promote Tweets to start conversations about your brand. You pay for the initial engagement.

- **Gain followers:** Promote your Twitter account and pay per follower gained.

- Increa**se brand awareness:** Promote your Tweets to a broad audience and pay for impressions (CPM).

- **Video views:** Promote your videos to a targeted audience and pay per video view.

- **App installs or re-engagement:** Promote your Tweets and pay per click to open or install your app.

Audience considerations: Hootsuite states that two-thirds of all Twitter users are male. Twitter is big outside of the USA and Canada—there's major growth happening in India, and Brazil, Japan, and Mexico are all big markets.

Two types of ads are offered on Twitter:

- Twitter Promote
- Twitter Ad Campaigns

Twitter Promote

Twitter promoting is used to promote 10 daily organic Tweets based on your specific audience. Providing they pass the Twitter quality filter. Focus on 5 interests or metro locations Twitter will do the rest.

Tip: The cost is USD 99 per month. An average of 30,000 accounts is reached, with an average gain of 30 new followers during the campaign.

Twitter Ad Campaigns

Ad campaigns are set up by choosing a business objective. This will allow your company to align its branding goals with the campaign objective. You can select existing organic Tweets to promote or create Tweets specifically as ads.

Tip: The best results come from running a separate campaign for mobile and desktop users. Twitter recommends you avoid using hashtags and @ mentions in your ads so that your audience does not click away.

Snapchat Ads

Snapchat assists with three types of marketing objectives:

- Awareness: Reach and engage with a large audience.
- Consideration: Push visits to websites, videos, or other content.
- Drive action: Drive newsletter sign-ups, app installs, foot traffic to your offline business, and more concrete actions.

Audience considerations: The volume of users on Snapchat is overwhelmingly the younger population. 78 percent of Snapchat users are 18-to-24-years old, compared to only 26 percent of 30-to-49-year-olds.

Three types of advertising tools are offered to help meet your objective.

Snapchat Ads Manager

The Ads Manager allows you to create a photo or video campaigns that appear between stories on the app. Ads run full-screen, vertical format, and include attachments for app installs, lead generation, video views, and website visits.

Tip: Newsfeeds run fast on Snapchat, which means users must keep the video to 3 to 5 seconds or less. Keep it simple and direct to the point! Use a powerful call-to-action and a key message.

Snapchat Filter Tool

Snapchat filters are graphic overlays that can be applied to Snaps. Snapchatters use them on average three billion times per day.

Tip: When using filers, make sure to provide context, for example, the time, place, and purpose of your campaign. Leave room for Snapchatters' images to shine—only use the top and/or bottom quarters of the screen for your filter creative.

Snap Publisher

The Publisher tool allows users to build an ad from scratch on a browser. It is a valuable tool for small businesses that don't have a large marketing team. Templates are provided, minimizing the need for a graphic design expert.

Story Ads

The ad forms a branded tile in the user's discover feed. It leads to a collection of 3-20 Snaps. It allows advertisers to provide a better platform to display products, services, or special offers. Attachments include a call-to-action, so users can swipe up to watch a trailer, install an app, or buy a product.

Tip: Supply the users with a tease line. Show them how they can benefit from your product.

According to Hootsuite, nearly 88% of users viewing Snapchat ads for a men's deodorant campaign were 13 to 34 years old. Millennials make up almost ¼ of the U.S. population. That's 80 million Americans spending $200 billion each year.

LinkedIn Ads

LinkedIn is the world's largest business stage. It makes sense to target goods dollar to dollar. The following steps will have you mastering LinkedIn like a breeze.

Objectives:

- Build brand awareness
- Drive website traffic
- Generate leads and convert prospects

Audience considerations: Business owners have rated LinkedIn as the best platform for B2B lead generation. LinkedIn is a professional networking platform. It offers targeting options based on professional qualifications like job title and seniority.

LinkedIn Ad Types

- Sponsored Content
- Sponsored InMail
- Text Ads

Sponsored Content

These ads will show in the news feed on mobile and desktop devices. The results expose content to a larger audience and give you the ability to showcase your brand.

Tip: Keep headlines under 150 characters, and use larger images to gain higher click-through rates. The recommended sizes are 1200 x 627 pixels.

According to Hootsuite, "The customer service software company Aspect used Sponsored Content to promote its thought leadership articles. The campaign increased Company Page followers by 17 percent and referral traffic to the Aspect blog by four times." (Hootsuite, n.d.)

Sponsored InMail

If you chose a sponsored mail option, the user can reach beyond the clients' news feed. The ads are sent through the inbox, and it's one way to deliver personalized messages. You can also use call-to-action buttons.

Ads Reach

- Attract more leads
- Have more and better conversations
- Send personalized invites to webinars and other events
- Target promotions to the right audience
- Promote content like downloadable eBooks and white papers

Tip: The best results come when body text is under 500 characters. The top five performing calls-to-action for Sponsored InMail are: Try, Free, Today, Click, and Apply.

Text Ads

These campaigns are a wonderful way to drive traffic to your LinkedIn Company page or website. They are similar to Google or Bing search ads.

For any business, it's best to create variations of the same ad. For example, clone the ad and then change the headline, slightly. Once the ad runs for some time, it will show the results and grant the ability to refine the specs. However, these ads only run on desktops, so it is a great way to attract busy professionals glancing at the news feed.

Ads Reach

- Fast and easy to get started
- Set your budget
- Choose your audience with laser-sharp B2B filters
- Track conversions
- Choose your model: cost-per-click or cost-per-thousand-impressions

Despite the name, text ads can include a thumbnail image of 50 x 50 pixels.

Tip: Use a human face such as a profile image for the best results.

Pinterest Ads

Pinterest ads have 5 types of business objectives:

- Build brand awareness
- Create audience engagement
- Drive traffic to your website

- Drive app installs
- Drive video impressions

Audience considerations: According to Hootsuite, "Pinterest has significantly more female users than males. According to the Pew Research Center, 41 percent of U.S. women use Pinterest, compared to just 16 percent of U.S. men. Because people use Pinterest to save ideas, it's a network that naturally leads to shopping and purchases, but those purchases may not happen right away." (Hootsuite, n.d.)

The ads are called Promoted Pins and look like normal Pins. The difference here is, you pay for them to be seen by a larger audience. Ads are identified with a small Promoted tag.

Tip: If users save your ads to their boards, the promoted label disappears, but you gain free organic impressions.

Two options are offered for pin promotion:

- Pinterest Ads Manager
- Promote Button

Pinterest Ads Manager

Start in the ads manager to create the Pinterest ad campaign. Align the advertising strategy with your business goals, including PPC or per impression. There is also an option to choose what network your ad appears on, browsing, or search.

Tip: Pinterest has a longer lead time than some other social media. It is best to run ads tied to a season or specific date, usually about 45 days in advance. Get creative with the DIY nature of the platform.

Promote Button

Pinterest states the promote button can be used to create an ad in only 9 seconds. Go to your profile, select a Pin, click the button, and set the daily budget. Promoted Pins are always PPC. Add some keywords and click once again. The ad will run on its own.

Tip: Start with promoting some of the best-performing Pins to get an idea of the market. Adjust as necessary, just track the results for future campaigns. When promoted Pins are saved, it expands organically.

YouTube Ads

YouTube offers unique options for running ads. It's quite different from the usual PPC or paid campaign. The options are vast and offer some specific creative constraints. But, it's important to know the knowledge base before investing in marketing.

Business Objectives:

- Collect leads
- Drive website traffic
- Build brand awareness and extend your reach
- Increase product and brand consideration
- Attract new viewers
- Grow your subscriber base

Audience considerations: According to HubSpot, "YouTube is the only social network used by more men than women. The difference is not huge: 75 percent of American men use YouTube, and 72 percent of American women. But this may be of interest if you're specifically targeting a male audience." (Hubspot, n.d.)

Video Ad Formats

Google owns YouTube, therefore you must have a Google Ads account to create the ads. There are two types of ads:

- TrueView In-Stream Ads
- TrueView Discovery Ads

The ads appear during any video that streams. Users have the option to skip the ad after 5 seconds. The recommended length is 12 seconds up to 3 minutes. Again, keep is simple!

Tip: If you're in the US or the UK, YouTube will send a professional filmmaker to shoot your 30-second ad if you commit to spending $350 on YouTube ads.

TrueView Discovery Ads

These ads appear on the YouTube homepage. Users must click the video to start watching. It is recommended to have a compelling thumbnail to grab the viewers' attention.

As an example, "The mattress company Tuft & Needle uses YouTube video ads to highlight how they're different from traditional mattress manufacturers. They target people searching for relevant keywords and dedicate half their Google ads budget to YouTube video because they're so happy with the results."

Bumper Ads

These ads must be less than 6 seconds and cannot be skipped. They play when someone starts viewing a video.

Tip: One strong point here is to just grab the viewers' attention. Include one message and leave time for the call-action button.

Chapter Twelve:

Graphic Design

The Vark Model shows us that the human brain is 90% visual. "It is estimated that 40% of people prefer visual learning over auditory or kinaesthetic," Neil Fleming. Therefore, graphic design is more than just pictures, graphs, or drawings. It is a crucial form of communication and problem solving for most humans. In the business world, it's an effective element to use to engage with consumers.

Graphic design is essential to building brand awareness, which in turn influences the customer's decision-making process. Below are some elements involved in quality graphic design:

2. Call to action (CTA): Persuading an action
3. Infographic: Sparks an interest
4. Blog post graphics: Visual content

Essentially, graphic design is an appealing way for companies to interact with their audience, hence the reason for social media's success. Design elements within content marketing will help sway prospects to learn more about your product, funneling conversation.

In conclusion, humans are visual creatures; when the brain stores detail it's done in two ways, verbal and visual. But when considering these factors in your marketing plan, consider that people don't recall decorative or arbitrary images, so you must illustrate something memorable to the person. This means the message will be committed to memory.

Affordable Graphic Design Tools

- Canva: Creative Platform for Graphic Designers
- Pic Monkey: Photo Editing and Design Website
- Inkscape: A powerful vector graphics tool that's free and open-source
- Krita: Free software packed with advanced drawing aids and templates
- GIMP: An incredible tool for any designer who works with photos
- Blender: The ultimate free tool for graphic designers creating 3D content

- Easel.ly: Online web tool to create visual infographics

Chapter Thirteen:

Grants & Loans for Entrepreneurs

"The amount of new business being launched in the United States grows dramatically. According to the US Small Business Administration (US Small Business Administration, n.d.) (SBA), in 2010 there were 27.9 million small companies in the U.S. Of those businesses, 75% were operated by one person alone. However, the odds of success lasting longer than 5 years are limited. In 10 years only 1/3 of them remain in operation. Despite these statistics small to mid-size mature businesses flourish—like Apple and Hewlett Packard, were born in a garage. We all know how those companies turned out."

Before any business can be successful or become a legend, it must have a consistent profit or access to financing.

SBA states, "The average startup for most business in the U.S. is about 30,000." (Small Business Administration, n.d.)You can use the cost calculator provided by Entrepreneur.com. This number may seem high, but there is a wide range of options when it comes to financing startups. Below is a list of ways for a new business to raise money:

- Self-Financing: Using personal funds to start a business.
  a) Personal savings
  b) Sell personal assets
  c) Credit cards
  d) Second mortgage or home equity loan
  e) Bank loan
  f) Cash retirement accounts
- Friends or Family
- Small Business Admin Loans (SBA)
  a) Loan program
  b) Microloans
- Venture Capital
- Angel Investors:
  a) Go4Funding
  b) MicroVentures
  c) Tech Coast Angels
  d) Investors' Circle
  e) Golden Seeds LLC
  f) Band of Angels

g) Hyde Park Angels

h) Alliance of Angels

i) Angel Capital Association

- Crowdfunding

  a) EquityNet

  b) SeedUps

  c) peerbackers

  d) RocketHub

  e) SeedInvest

- Peer to Peer Loans

  a) Incubators

  b) Idealab

In conclusion, preparing a start-up business requires an extensive amount of planning and effort. It is an option that must be weighed carefully, considering all the benefits and downsides of the funding options. Many small businesses are started using multiple sources of funding, which allows some flexibility. In the event of an unexpected financial expense, the funding will be there to solve the problem. Fortunately, the amount of new fund sources is growing constantly, making it an even better time to start your own business.

Outsourcing

One way to manage a lack of employees or a high workload is to outsource labor. This has been a common practice for many years, although with the invention of the Internet, outsourcing has taken on new levels of profitability. It has become a great alternative to many companies who need small important jobs done in a short period.

Outsourcing simply means the practice of obtaining goods or services from an alternative source, usually outside your home country. The costs will vary depending on the job. Companies outsource for several reasons, but two of the biggest motivations are lower costs and profitability. The strategy is very helpful to small business owners who have a limited budget and need to have quality work done for a lower price.

Leadership Team and Communication

"Few things help an individual more than to place responsibility on them and let them know you trust them" *Booker T. Washington.*

One key role of any leader is the ability to use effective communication. The messages must come from respect and trust, and this is what separates a good leader from a poor leader. Interactions need to be frequent and constructive, which will encourage a healthy, productive workplace.

Positive communication is important in any area of life; between family members, spouses, co-workers, bosses, etc. Without conversation, productivity slows, and spats over expectations increase. Below are ways to create effective communication habits in the workplace:

1. Open meetings
2. Emails
3. One on one conversations
4. Amenable atmosphere
5. Communication training
6. Confidence in the staff
7. Simple clarifying expectations
8. Use visuals
9. Listen to feedback
10. Use positive body language
11. Eliminate unnecessary repetition
12. Maintain a positive tone

13. Use humor when appropriate

14. Be articulate

15. Give positive affirmations

The goal of any good leader should be to communicate in an effective manner that is respectful by constructively sharing your thoughts and feelings with the team or staff. The next step of good communication is the ability to listen to feedback from the team and staff. Then make the appropriate decision based on the proper information.

Chapter Fourteen

Setting Up a Business

According to Small Business, "There are more than 28 million small businesses in the United States, making up a whopping 99.7 percent of all U.S. businesses, according to the Small Business Administration. When you consider some of the most popular reasons to start a business, including having a unique business idea, designing a career that has the flexibility to grow with you, working toward financial independence, and investing in yourself — it's no wonder that small businesses are everywhere." (Small Business, n.d.)

Below are four steps to start a business:

Step 1: Research

Whether you have already identified a business idea or not, take some time to research your options.

- Weight the odds
- Does the idea have the potential to succeed?
- Do you have the resources to start this endeavor?

You will need to run your business idea through a validation process before you go any further. The only way a small business will prosper is if it can solve a problem, fulfill a demand, or create something the market needs.

Luckily, several options are available to identify the answer, including focus groups and even trial and error. As you explore the market, some of the questions you should answer include:

- Is there a need for your anticipated products/services?
- Who needs it?
- Are there other companies offering similar products/services now?
- What is the competition like?
- How will your business fit into the market?

Step 2: Plan

A business plan is the blueprint of any business start-up. Once you have created this plan, the business can form its identity. The good news is that there are different types of business plans for different types of businesses.

If the plan is to seek financial support from an investor, a traditional plan must be in place. Business plans are generally thorough and have a common set of sections that investors and banks look for when they are validating your idea. Otherwise, a simple one-page business plan will be sufficient. In fact, using notepad in Microsoft can hold a plan that will be improved upon over time. Having any plan in writing is a great way to start.

Step 3: Plan Finances

Many people are afraid to start a business due to a lack of finances, but in this digital age, many options that did not exist before the Internet have opened.

Create a budget planner that includes all start-up costs such as licenses and permits, equipment, legal fees, insurance, branding, market research, inventory, trademarking, grand opening events, property leases, etc. Include expenses you anticipate over the next year, like rent, utilities, marketing and advertising, production, supplies, travel expenses, employee salaries, your salary, etc. It is important to be realistic about your profits, so plan for the yearly investment, but hope for the best.

Once the numbers are calculated, below are some ways to fund the small business:

- Financing
- Small business loans
- Small business grants
- Angel investors
- Crowdfunding

Bootstrapping is another way to fund the business. Start with a small amount and use it as necessary. However, you figure out the plan, so use the methods that best fit your needs.

Step 4: Create a Business Structure

Your small business can be a sole proprietorship, a partnership, a limited liability company (LLC), or a corporation. The business entity you choose will impact many factors, from your business name to your liability, to how you file your taxes. As the business grows the initial structure can be adjusted.

Depending on the complexity of your business, it may be worth investing in a consultation from an attorney or CPA to ensure you are making the right structure choice for your business.

Business Structure

There are 6 common business structures:

- Sole Proprietorship
- Partnership
- Corporation
- S Corporation
- Limited Liability (LLC)
- Limited Liability (LLP)

The tax implications vary greatly, so choose wisely. Be sure it matches your business needs.

Sole Proprietorship

A sole proprietor is someone who owns an unincorporated business by himself or herself. However, if you are the sole member of a domestic limited liability company (LLC), you are not a sole proprietor if you elect to treat the LLC as a corporation. If you intend to work alone, this structure may be the answer.

The tax aspects of a sole proprietorship are appealing because the expenses and your income from the business are included on your income tax return, Form 1040. Profits and losses are recorded on a form called Schedule C, which is filled with a 1040. The amount from Schedule C is then transferred to your tax return. However, the self-employment tax percentages are high, so prepare for the expense during tax season. It does offer business losses that may offset income earned from other sources.

The federal government permits you to pay estimated taxes in four equal amounts throughout the year on the 15th of April, June, September, and January. In a sole proprietorship, earnings are taxed only once, unlike other business structures. Also, you will have complete control over your business - you make all the decisions.

Raising money for a sole proprietorship can be difficult. Banks and other financing sources may be reluctant to make business loans to sole proprietorships. In most cases, you will have to depend on your financing sources, such as savings, home equity, or family loans.

Partnership

Business ventures operated by several individuals should consider a partnership. Partnerships come in two varieties: general partnerships and limited partnerships. In a general partnership, the partners manage the company and assume responsibility for the partnership's debts and other obligations. A limited partnership has both general and limited partners. The general partners own and operate the business and assume liability for the partnership, while the limited partners serve as investors only; they have no control over the company and are not subject to the same liabilities as of the general partners.

If you don't expect to have many passive investors, a limited partnership is usually not the best choice for new business due to all the filings and administrative complexities. If you have two or more partners who want to be actively involved, a general partnership would be much easier to form.

One of the major advantages of a partnership is the tax treatment it enjoys. A partnership does not pay tax on its income but "passes through" any profits or losses to the individual partners. At tax time, the partnership must file a tax return (Form 1065) that reports its income and loss to the IRS. Besides, each partner reports his or her share of income and loss on Schedule K-1 of Form 1065.

The personal liability if you use a general partnership in the business requires each general partner to act on behalf of the partnership, take out loans and make decisions that will affect and be binding on all the partners (if the partnership agreement permits). Partnerships require legal accounting services and usually are more expensive to operate.

Corporation

In general, a corporation is formed under state law by the filing of articles of incorporation with the state. The state must generally date-stamp the articles before they are effective. You may wish to consult the law of the state in which the organization is incorporated. A corporation is an independent legal entity, separate from its owners, and as such it requires complying with more regulations and tax requirements.

One of the benefits of incorporation is liability protection. The business is its own identity; in other words, the business pays taxes and you are an employee. A corporation also can retain some of its profits without the owner paying tax on them.

Corporations can raise money, and sell the stock, either common or preferred, to raise funds.

Corporations also continue indefinitely, even if one of the shareholders dies, sells the shares, or becomes disabled. The corporate structure, however, comes with several downsides. A major one is higher costs. Corporations are formed under the laws of each state with its own set of regulations. You will probably need the assistance of an attorney to guide you. In addition, because a corporation must follow more complex rules and regulations than a partnership or sole proprietorship, it requires more accounting and tax preparation services.

Corporations also pay double taxes on business earnings. They are subject to corporate tax with both state and federal, but the shareholders that are paid dividends are taxed on the individual tax rates.

A corporation is not required to pay tax on earnings paid as reasonable compensation, and it can deduct the payments as a business expense. However, the IRS has limits on what it believes to be reasonable compensation.

S Corporation

S corporations are corporations that elect to pass corporate income, losses, deductions, and credits through to their shareholders for federal tax purposes. Shareholders of S corporations report the flow-through of income and losses on their tax returns and are assessed tax at their individual income tax rates. This allows S corporations to avoid double taxation on corporate income. S corporations are responsible for tax on certain built-in gains and passive income at the entity level.

If S corporations don't have inventory, they can use the cash method for accounting. The process is simplified. Income is taxable when received and expenses are deductible when paid.

S corporations can also have up to 100 shareholders. This option allows them to have more investors, and in essence gain more investors.

The downside is they are subject to many of the same rules as corporations, which means higher legal and tax services. They also must file articles of incorporation, hold directors and shareholders meetings, keep corporate minutes, and allow shareholders to vote on major corporate decisions.

The major difference between a regular corporation and an S corporation is that S corporations can only issue one class of stock. This can hamper a company's ability to raise any capital.

Limited Liability Company

S corporations are corporations that elect to pass corporate income, losses, deductions, and credits through to their shareholders for federal tax purposes. Shareholders of S corporations report the flow-through of income and losses on their tax returns and are assessed tax at their individual income tax rates. This allows S corporations to avoid double taxation on corporate income. S corporations are responsible for tax on certain built-in gains and passive income at the entity level.

Yes, they are similar however, an LLC offers owners more benefits than S corporations. The shareholder limit is 100, plus any member is allowed full partaking in business operations.

The set-up of an LLC requires filing articles of incorporation with the secretary of state but is generally much easier than a corporation. Some state statutes stipulate that the company must dissolve after 30 years. Technically, the company dissolves when a member dies, quits, or retires.

With a limited liability partnership, members are liable for their malpractice insurance. The legal form works well for those involved in professional practice, such as physicians.

Once settled on a business structure, the circumstances that make one type of business organization favorable are always subject to changes in the laws. It makes sense to reassess your form of business from time to time to make sure you are using the one that provides the most benefits.

Step 5: Pick and Register Business Name

A major factor in starting a business is choosing the right name. It plays a role in almost every area of business. Choose wisely!

After you have chosen a name, the next step is checking to see if it's trademarked or currently in use. The name must be registered, and a sole proprietor needs to register the name with the state or county clerk. Corporations, LLCs, or limited partnerships typically register their business name when the formation paperwork is filed.

Once the name is registered, search for the domain name. It may be best to check on available domain names ahead of time. It is recommended to have three different options in case the first choice is not available. Online presence in this digital age is imperative.

Step 6: Get Licenses and Permits

Any business start-up requires paperwork. Depending on the choice of business the licensing or permits will vary. The location will also determine the type of paperwork. Always research what is needed ahead of time to help eliminate any surprises.

Step 7: Choose an Accounting System

Any business must have an accounting system in place beforehand. However, for small business, this is extremely important. The system will manage a budget, set rates and pricing, conduct business, and file taxes. If you are unsure of the mechanics, the option to hire an accountant is always a good alternative.

Step 8: Set Up Business Location

All businesses need a dedicated location of operation. Not only for tax purposes but to maintain a professional atmosphere. Once the location is decided, then it's time to get all the equipment involved in running the business. Equipment can be purchased or leased.

Step 9: Initiate a Team

Once all the particulars are completed, it's time to either hire full-time employees or part-time staff members. The Small Business Administration has an excellent guide to hiring your first employee that is useful for new small business owners.

If you are not hiring employees but instead are outsourcing work to independent contractors, now is the time to work with an attorney to get your independent contractor agreement in place and start your search.

In conclusion, if you are a true solopreneur, you may not need employees or contractors. Although, having a support team is important. The staff can be mentors, friends, or small business coaches, whoever services the purpose of your business needs.

Step 10: Business Promotion

Now that the hard initial work is done, it is time to start attracting clients or customers. The process begins with writing a unique selling proposition. Create a marketing plan! Without income, the business won't survive. Then, explore as many small business marketing ideas as possible to promote the business most effectively.

What is Copyrighting?

A copyright is the protection of an original work of authorship, both published and unpublished. It is used by writers, musicians, artists, and others to protect their work from unauthorized commercial use.

Understanding Copyright Protection

Automatically acquire the copyright of your work the moment you create it. Your work is automatically protected by copyright when it is "fixed in a tangible form" like a piece of writing or drawing on a piece of paper. This means the U.S. copyright laws apply to your work as soon as you produce it, write it, record it, or draw it. An idea or invention can only be protected when it is in tangible form. Write the idea out in detail.

In situations where you authorized a person to record your words, you hold the 'first of record,' as you remain the author. But it would be advisable to have them sign a non-disclosure agreement.

U.S. law prohibits copyrighting a recording of a live public performance unless you obtain permission from the performers. You could be sued for infringement for making it or sharing it online or anywhere else.

Understand the difference between a copyright, a patent, and a trademark. Copyright protects original works of authorship created by you. However, a patent protects inventions and useful discoveries. A trademark protects distinctive words, phrases, symbols, sounds, and designs. Trademarks identify and distinguish the source of the goods (and services) of one party from those of another party.

It is important to know what types of work are protected by copyrights. Copyright protects original, tangible work you have created including things like writings, drawings, photographs, books, and poems.

It also protects:

- Movies and soundtracks
- Choreography and dramatic works
- Songs and sound recordings

- Artistic works like paintings and sculptures and computer software programs
- Architecture plans and drawings

Copyrights do not protect an idea or something expressed verbally. Copyright also does not protect:

- Facts or concepts
- Domain names
- Slogans
- Systems or methods of operation
- Names (including band names) or titles
- Works created by the US government
- Works in the "public domain", i.e., having an expired or void US copyright.

The ownership of copyright affords an exclusive right to make copies of protected work. An owner can sell, print, or distribute the work legally. Copyright also allows you to create adaptations, translations, or derivative pieces from your work, and to perform your work.

However, the exclusive rights come with limitations, such as fair use, first sale, or certain educational and non-profit uses.

Anyone can choose to authorize others, via license, to exercise some or all your exclusive rights either for compensation or as a courtesy. The prevention of others from making personal copies is not prohibited. Only the use of commercial use can be regulated.

Work for hire can be made for an employer or a client under an independent contract. The law determines who the original owner of the copyright is, which also determines the copyright duration. If a work is created by an employee as part of their work, then the employer is considered "the author" and owns the copyright.

If an independent contractor is hired, make sure the copyright agreement is determined before the start of the project. Complex issues arise when collaborating with others in a jointly authored work. Research when copyright protection ends.

You must know when copyright protection ends. For works created in 1978 or later, copyright generally lasts for the duration of the last living author's life, plus an additional 70 years. If the work was made for hire, anonymous, or created under a pseudonym, the copyright lasts for 95 years from the first publication or 120 years from the creation.

Copyright will last beyond the normal lifespan of a person, so the necessary paperwork should be initiated while the person is alive. The material should be kept with a will or estate plan. Ownership can also be transferred by contacting the US copyright office.

 Until 1972, sound recordings were not protected by copyrights, but may be protected under various state laws until 2067. Foreign copyright laws vary.

Registering a Copyright

1) Copyrights are a consideration for anyone, but not necessary. They can be registered through the U.S. Copyright office. Several reasons apply for copyright registration:
    - A registered copyright is a matter of public record.
    - Registered copyright holders receive a certificate of registration from the U.S. Copyright Office.
    - Registration must be done to bring a lawsuit on a related infringement.

- Any works registered may be eligible for statutory damages and attorney's fees.

The process must be completed within the first 5 years of publication. Otherwise, the burden falls on the author to prove ownership.

2) Copyrights can be registered online very easily. Visit the U.S. Copyright Office's online registration site. You will need to register an account with the office to start your application. A digital version of the work must be provided, or you can request a shipping label.

   Then, pay the filing fees and submit all works. You can also pay the filing fee online and submit your application.

3) Register your copyright by mail. If you chose to register by mail, the U.S. Copyright Office website can provide the proper paperwork. If you are registering a novel, select the Literary Form (Form TX), a music or voice recording, select the Sound Recording Form (Form SR).

   Print the form and refer to the guide as to the number of copies that are required. Make a copy or copies of your copyrighted work.

Once the application is received, you will get a certificate in the mail, or online if that route is chosen. If for any reason the application is rejected, a notification with the issue will be mailed. You will have a chance to appeal.

Part Three: Protecting a Copyright

1) Place notices on all copyrighted work. A notice is helpful in case of infringement. A copyright notice may also make it easier to collect damages in any potential infringement lawsuit.

   A copyright notice should contain the word "copyright" or a "c" in a circle (©), along with the date of first publication and the name of the owner of the copyright

   If someone copies a copyrighted work, send a cease and desist letter before taking any legal action. The letter must include details of the issue, and ask the party to stop their illegal actions. From there if the issue persists, consult an attorney for further options.

Chapter Fifteen:

Online TV Stations – YouTube, IGTV, or Facebook Live

The popularity of online TV stations has rapidly increased over the past several years. The various channels offer a wide variety of entertainment and give people the chance to connect with like-minded individuals within the security of their homes.

Humans are social beings that need contact with other people regularly. Now with the advent of the Internet, we can easily communicate with cultures all over the world. We can stay in touch with old friends and family, or meet new colleagues all around the world.

Online TV entertainment or business channels are easy to distribute and contain a wide diversity of information. It can be accessed by the general public or smaller groups of similar interests. Most distribution is free or minimal cost, making it possible for anyone to succeed in making money online, or for businesses to reach a greater audience.

Instagram – IGTV

IGTV was designed for watching long-form vertical videos from your favorite creators. According to Instagram, teens are watching 40% less TV in recent years, however online TV viewing has increased dramatically.

One drawback of IGTV is that the video is often incompatible with certain smartphones; horizontal options are very limited. IGTV videos start playing automatically when you open the app. It pulls content from the people you already follow, so no one must hunt for videos you might enjoy.

However, if you want to search there are 4 sections available:

1) You
2) Following
3) Continue Watching
4) Popular

Anyone can also choose to follow specific creators, and the recommendations will be offered the next time you sign into the app.

Google - YouTube

YouTube was created in 2005 and has become one of the most popular sites on the web. According to GCF Global visitors watch around 6 billion hours every month. YouTube makes it simple to watch online or create and upload your videos from virtually anywhere. The videos can be saved and shared with anyone connected to the Internet.

One of the main reasons YouTube is so popular is the vast number of videos available to visitors. YouTube states that on average, 100 hours of video are uploaded every minute. So, there is always something new to watch. Another valid reason to use this channel is that it's centered around user-generated content.

Facebook Live

Facebook took the Internet by storm when it was presented and now the same giant offers Facebook Live. This gives verified VIP users the ability to broadcast online using the Facebook Mentions app. Streams show on the news feed, allowing users to comment in real-time.

Since the release of Facebook Live, the popularity expanded, overcoming Vimeo by 78% in 2018. It is no surprise it's so attractive since Facebook has millions of users online regularly around the world.

Marketing professionals are finding Facebook Live widely popular due to the simple application of uploading and using the channel to engage users. They can build authentic relationships with fans and followers in real-time. However, the channel has some important tricks that need to be learned to gain all the benefits of the platform.

Vimeo

The channel is stationed in NY, and although YouTube is the leading video sharing goliath, Vimeo is finding its way into the market. It was launched in 2004 by a group of filmmakers. They have grown their platform to over 80 million viewers. Granted, most of the creators are artists, filmmakers, musicians, or other areas of the media industry. The biggest difference between Vimeo and YouTube is the singularity of the creative art.

If you want a more refined viewing platform, YouTube has everything that someone can point a camera at, while Vimeo is specialized toward the creative arts. It's especially popular if you like video games.

For businesses that are geared towards the finer elements of media entertainment, Vimeo may be right up your alley. Depending on your audience, you might choose this alternative.

Chapter Sixteen:

How to Make Money on Social Media

Since the invention of the Internet, the ways people can make money have become limitless. One fantastic way to increase any income is social media. In fact, it can be very lucrative. Below are some outlets for making money through social media:

1. Endorse affiliate products
2. Create and promote information products
3. Sell products and services
4. Use visual media to promote your crafts
5. Offer coaching or consulting services
6. Join the YouTube partner program

We have only listed a few ways to generate extra income using social media, and there are many more options. The important thing to remember is the process may not be easy to get started and it will take time to become financially beneficial, but don't give up and be persistent.

Public Relations

The public relations business has gotten a bad rap over the years because most people do not understand what it means or what the job entails. Public relations promote a client's product or services in a manner free of charge to unpaid audiences. The idea is to generate a public understanding of the business's skills and industry in which they work. Below are 5 things every public relations person should know:

1. Public relations is like storytelling
   a) Write and distribute press releases
   b) Write speeches
   c) Write pitches (less formal than press releases) about a firm and send them directly to journalists
   d) Create and execute special events designed for public outreach and media relations
   e) Conduct market research on the firm or the firm's messaging

f) Expand business contacts via personal networking or attendance and sponsoring at events

g) Write and blog for the web (internal or external sites)

h) Create public relations crisis management strategies

i) Design social media promotions and responses to negative opinions online

2. Public relations is different than advertising
3. Understand the nature of the news
   a) Create the story
   b) Follow a story
4. Social media cannot replace traditional media
5. It is possible to measure public relations

Media is Your Friend

Media is an essential part of marketing any business. If people do not know you exist, how can they become clients?

Below are 28 ways to help get media attention for your business:

1. Learn what media outlets are covering

2. Use email over the phone
3. Engage the right people
4. Schedule regular postings, stories, and engagement
5. Become the expert
6. Always be reachable
7. Create a resource center for your business
8. Tweet with followers
9. Take advantage of freebies
10. Plan special events in your local area and invite the media
11. Engage on social media platforms
12. Offer to review products that pertain to your business
13. Write a complete press release
14. Be a resource for clients or followers
15. Avoid buzzwords and tech jargon
16. Use bullet points and pitches
17. Don't overhype
18. Do something unique
19. Create research
20. Give shout outs
21. Invite the media to your special events

22. Start with blogs of media outlets
23. Create your media shortlist
24. Attend community events where the press may be present
25. Watch publications with smaller and more targeted readerships
26. Hold a fundraising drive
27. Carefully choose your backdrop
28. Learn from your experience

Social Media Marketing Tools

- **Sensible** is a scheduling tool for social media **(My Personal Favorite)**
- **Buffer** is a scheduling tool for social media.
- **Buzzsumo** is a research tool that tells you how your content is doing and who's spreading the word.
- **Missinglettr** helps you automate the process of creating social content by scraping your blog post content and creating a year's worth of social content for you. It makes nine individual posts dripped out to your social channels over a year.
- **MeetEdgar** is your handy automated content manager.
- **Hootsuite** handles multiple social media accounts, bringing them under one login into a single dashboard.
- **Mention** is an extremely comprehensive social listening tool.

- Sumo has a whole suite of useful traffic and social media tools that can help improve your marketing strategy.
- IFTTT means if this, then that. This tool lets you set up rules that make running your social media marketing empire much easier.
- Zapier is another tool that encourages automation and does share some similarities with IFTTT.
- Bitly is a link shortener, taking lengthy URLs and shrinking them into much smaller ones.
- Sprout Social provides engagement, publishing, analytics, and team collaboration tools.
- Canva makes it easy to create gorgeous infographics, cover images, and thumbnails for your social media accounts.
- Design Wizard is another tool that's good for making visual content, with a reasonably simple and intuitive interface.
- Socialbakers enables brands to work smart on social media through artificial intelligence (AI) to understand audience behavior.

- **Hootsuite** is a social media marketing tool that can help you manage all your social media accounts from a single dashboard.
- **Post Planner** makes it easy for you to find and share content consistently to get predictable, considerable, and remarkable results on social media.
- **Sprinklr** is a four-in-one social media marketing platform that can help you with social engagement, social advocacy, customer care, and social advertising.
- **Followerwonk** is a useful tool on the list that you can exclusively use with Twitter.
- **SocialFlow** allows you to schedule your posts when your target audience is active and engage in real-time.
- **Brand24** gives you insights on what people are saying online about your brand. This tool helps you track your competitors, too.
- **Tweepi** is an AI-powered social media marketing tool that helps you grow your brand's presence on Twitter.

- **Tracx** is the only social listening tool that provides an all-in-one solution that captures the full conversation.

- **ManyChat** is an easy tool that can help you create a Facebook messenger bot to provide marketing and sales support to consumers.

- **Facebook Ads Manager** is a Facebook tool that helps you create and manage Facebook ads.

- **Fanpage Karma** is a multi-functional tool for Facebook management.

- **Heyo** is a Facebook marketing tool that can help you get more leads. It can help you create sweepstakes, contests, and hashtag campaigns for Facebook. You can use pre-made templates.

- **Likealyzer** is a very simple Facebook marketing tool that helps you optimize the performance of your Facebook Page.

- **Pagemodo** is a great Facebook marketing tool. It has an intuitive editor that helps you modify and build up your Facebook pages. You can customize your Facebook business page with impressive cover photos, add custom tabs, and create contests for engagement.

- **ShortStack** has positioned itself as the most powerful marketing platform for contests and giveaways.
- **MobileMonkey** is an effective messenger marketing tool that helps you create Facebook Messenger chatbots and automate marketing and support tasks.

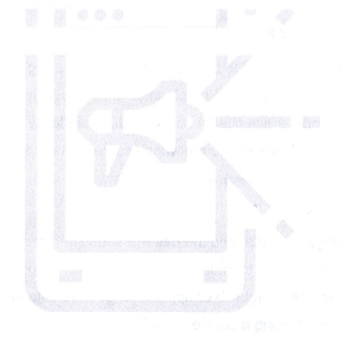

Social Media Directory

A.

Abandonment rate: The percentage of social customer service issues that customers abandon before they are resolved.

Algorithm: A rules-based procedure for making calculations or solving problems—they're everywhere in computer science! In social media, constantly shifting algorithms control which contents its users see (and don't see), as well as what topics and hashtags are trending.

Analytics: Data, and the patterns found in that data, are often used to make marketing or advertising decisions. A website or application gathers data for its analytics using a cookie or other tracking tag that monitors users' behavior. The tag activates when users begin their visits and then stores data about what pages they visited, what actions they completed, and how they interacted with different elements such as clicking on buttons or performing a search.

Authenticity: The practice of using a tone and voice online that expresses who you are. For brands, being open and authentic on social media means a great deal to those who want to engage with you. Conveying your brand's values through your content and replies, and interacting with followers in a way that's relatable and human, all contribute to your sense of authenticity.

B.

Bio: The small portion of any digital profile that tells new or prospective followers who you are. All social platforms offer space to write a bio. It's the first thing users see when they discover your profile, and a good one can greatly improve how often you show up in keyword searches.

Bitly: Bitly is a free URL shortening service that provides statistics for the links users share online. Bitly is often used to condense long URLs to make them easier to share on social networks such as Twitter.

Block: A Twitter feature that allows you to prevent another user from:

- Following you
- Sliding into your DMs
- Adding you to their lists
- Tagging you in photos

Blocking a troublesome or harassing user allows you some peace—if they mention you, those tweets won't appear in your notifications, and the user receives a message letting them know they've been blocked.

However, Twitter cannot prevent anyone from seeing your public tweets. If you need someone out of your digital hair completely, use a protected account.

BoardReader: BoardReader is a free search engine that allows users to search for keywords only in posts and titles of online forums, a popular form of social networking.

Bookmarking: Bookmarking online follows the same idea of placing a bookmark in a physical publication - you're simply marking something you found important, enjoyed, or want to continue reading later. The only difference online is that it's happening through websites using one of the various bookmarking services available, such as Pocket, or right within your browser.

Brand advocate: A customer who loves your organization so much that they become an extension of your marketing team. They evangelize your products or services without being asked and can become even more valuable if you connect with them directly to engage and empower them.

Brandjacking: The hijacking of a person or organization's name or likeness to promote an agenda or damage the target's reputation. Brandjackers don't hack their targets' social accounts; instead, they assume a target's online identity with fake accounts, promoted hashtags, and satirical marketing campaigns.

C.

Chatbot: A type of bot that lives in messaging apps (such as Facebook Messenger) and uses artificial intelligence to perform tasks via simulated conversation. A chatbot can be used for customer service, data collection, and more. Facebook is one of the leaders in chatbot integration.

Click-through rate (CTR): A common metric for reporting on the number of people who viewed a piece of content then took an action, such as clicking on an ad or link. CTR is most commonly used for pay-per-click advertising and other performance-driven channels. The general philosophy is that the higher your CTR, the more effective your marketing is.

Community management: The practice of developing relationships around a common interest, done by monitoring and engaging with those who engage with the common interest. The goal is to nurture relationships so that the community acts as advocates on behalf of the common interest.

Competitor sentiment: The practice of monitoring how users feel about other organizations in your space through social media monitoring. Whether positive or negative, this intel can provide important context that helps you to make strategic business decisions to stay ahead of the competition.

Connections: The LinkedIn equivalent of a Facebook 'friend' is a 'connection.' Because LinkedIn is a social networking site, the people you are connecting with are not necessarily people you are friends with, but rather professional contacts that you've met, heard speak, done business with, or know through another connection. Connections are categorized by 1st degree, 2nd degree, and 3rd degree.

Content curation: The process of scouring the Internet for the best, most relevant content for an audience and then presenting it to them in a meaningful way. Unlike content marketing, content curation doesn't involve creating new content. Instead, it's about creating value for your audience by saving them time and effort. There's no shortage of content out there, but not all of it is worth reading. Organizing relevant content into pinboards, newsletters, or weekly roundups can help you build an audience and demonstrate your subject matter expertise.

Content management system (CMS): An online application that allows you to draft, edit, share, schedule, and index your content. Popular web content management systems have polished interfaces that allow you to publish content without knowing code. Hootsuite is a CMS.

Content marketing: The practice of attracting and retaining customers through the creation and distribution of valuable content, such as videos, white papers, guides, and infographics. Marketers hope to earn customer loyalty and influence decisions by publishing useful, entertaining, or educational content.

Conversion: A positive action taken on a website. The action demonstrates that the visitor is "raising their hand" and becoming a lead or customer. Sales are just one type of conversion; other examples include webinar registrations, newsletter signups, and gated-content downloads. Once a conversion takes place—usually involving the capture of a name and email address—a lead can be nurtured into a customer. In social marketing, conversion tracking is crucial to properly attribute revenue to social media efforts.

Cost per click (CPC): The terms pay-per-click (PPC) and cost-per-click (CPC) are sometimes used interchangeably, sometimes as distinct terms. When used as distinct terms, **PPC** indicates *payment* based on click-throughs, while **CPC** indicates *measurement* of cost on a per-click basis for contracts not based on click-throughs.

Creative Commons: Creative Commons is a nonprofit corporation dedicated to making it easier for people to share and build upon the work of others, consistent with the rules of copyright. It provides free licenses and other legal tools to mark creative work with the freedom the creator wants it to carry, so others can share, remix, use commercially, or any combination thereof.

Crowdsourcing: Leveraging your online community to assist in services, content, and ideas. Business applications for crowdsourcing include getting your audience to help translate your product or asking industry experts to contribute tips and tracks for an upcoming blog post.

D.

Dashboard: In a social relationship platform, a single screen where marketers can view their feeds, see and interact with ongoing conversations, monitor social trends, access analytics, and more.

Delicious: Delicious is a free online bookmarking service that lets users save website addresses publicly and privately online so they can be accessed from any device connected to the internet and shared with friends.

Digg: Digg is a social news website that allows members to submit and vote for articles. Articles with the most votes appear on the homepage of the site and subsequently are seen by the largest portion of the site's membership, as well as other visitors.

Direct message: A private Twitter or Instagram message. Direct messages can be sent only to Twitter and Instagram users who are already following you—and you can receive direct messages only from users you follow unless you have opted in to receiving direct messages from anyone in your user settings.

Disappearing content: Content that vanishes after a set amount of time (such as Snapchat, Facebook Stories, and Instagram Stories).

Display ad: Typically, small visual advertisements that are shown on websites. Common formats include images, Flash, video, and audio. They can also be text-based (for example, Google AdWords lets you build text-based display ads). In general, display ads are used for large audience-based media buys or retargeting.

E.

Embedded media: Digital media that is displayed outside of its native setting, such as within another piece of content (e.g., a GIF embedded into a Facebook comment, or a YouTube video shared in a Tweet).

Endorsement: An endorsement on LinkedIn refers to an instance in which another LinkedIn user recognizes you for one of the skills you have listed on your profile.

Engagement: Talking to, messaging, or otherwise interacting with other people on social networks. Engagement broadly encompasses many types of actions, from commenting on Instagram posts to producing a Facebook Live show with an open Q&A. Engagement is central to any social media strategy.

Engagement rate: The percentage of users who saw your social media post and took some kind of action (clicked the link, replied, shared, retweeted, etc.). The engagement rate is a valuable metric to gauge the success of your social media messaging. Twitter Analytics provides in-depth engagement rate data for every Tweet you send.

Eventbrite: Eventbrite is a provider of online event management and ticketing services. Eventbrite is free if your event is free. If you sell tickets to your event, Eventbrite collects a fee per ticket.

F.

Facebook fan: A user who likes your Facebook Page.

Facebook group: A space on Facebook where you can communicate and share content with a select group of people. There are three types of groups: public, closed, and secret. Make sure you understand the privacy settings of any group that you're a member and keep in mind that even in a closed or secret group, your information can still be copied, pasted, and shared. You can join a maximum of 6,000 Facebook groups.

Facebook Live: A Facebook feature that allows you to stream live video to your family, friends, and followers. You can get live reactions during your broadcast and interact with viewers in real-time.

Facebook notes A Facebook feature that enables users and brands to publish longer content to Facebook. Users can format their notes like blog posts with features such as header images, photos, quotes, links, and hashtags

Facebook Offers: A Facebook Ads feature that allows brands to share special deals and discounts with their social media audiences. Businesses can create online or offline (in-store) offers, and can share these in an Offers ad or a post on their Page.

Facebook Reach: The number of unique users who have seen content from your Facebook Page. Reach is not the same as impressions, which is the total number of times your content is viewed (including multiple views from the same user).

Facebook provides two different reach metrics:

Total Reach: the number of unique users who saw any content associated with your Page during the last seven days, including those who view your Page posts, visit your Page after searching for it, and see ads associated with your Page.

Post Reach: the number of unique users who have seen a particular Facebook Page post in their News Feed.

Facebook Reactions: Ways Facebook users can react to posts beyond a simple "like." Introduced in February 2015, current reactions include "love," "haha," "wow," "sad," and "angry." (We're campaigning for an "ewww" reaction, as well as an "eye roll.")

Facebook Town Hall: A Facebook feature that helps citizens connect and interact with their government representatives at the state, local, and federal levels. Users can look up their representatives by inputting their home address, and then use the Town Hall page to follow all their elected officials, get reminders to vote, and display a constituent badge on their comments when they post to a politician's page.

Facebook Watch: A video platform that features made-for-social TV shows and longer content on the social network everyone loves to hate.

Favorite: An indication that someone likes your Tweet, given by clicking the heart icon.

Feed: The social media data format that provides users with a steady stream of updates and information.

Filter: A photographic effect that can be applied to images before publishing them, from simple black-and-white or sepia to those ubiquitous flower crowns and puppy ears. Available on Instagram, Snapchat, Facebook Messenger, and many other apps with camera integrations, the popularity of filters has resulted in the hashtag #nofilter, a proud declaration that your latest photo is unedited.

First response time: The time it takes a company to give its first response to a customer's comment or inquiry on social media. This can be a key performance indicator for social customer service because even if the issue is not resolved immediately, a quick first response can demonstrate that a company is listening and willing to help.

Follow Friday (#ff) - Follow Friday is a trend via the hashtag #ff every Friday on Twitter. Users select other usernames and tweet them with #ff in their post, meaning they recommend following those Twitter users. There is debate about whether this trend is past its prime.

Follower: A Twitter user who has subscribed to your Twitter feed to see your tweets in their feed.

Followers-to-following ratio: The ratio of your social media followers to those you are following. In an ideal world, you have more followers than users you are following.

Friendship page: A page that tells the story of a relationship between two people connected on Facebook. Facebook Friendship pages display a variety of content, including photos that both people are tagged in together, public messages that they have exchanged, and their mutual friends and interests.

G.

Geotagging: Adding a specific location to a photo, video, or social media message. The ubiquity of GPS-enabled smartphones has made geotagging a core aspect of social media.

Geotargeting: A feature on many social media platforms that allows users to share their content with geographically defined audiences. Instead of sending a generic message for the whole world to see, you can refine the messaging and language of your content to better connect with people in specific cities, countries, and regions. You can also filter your audience by language.

GIF: Pronounced "gif," with a hard G, no matter what the actual creator of the GIF says. An acronym for Graphics Interchange Format, which refers to a file format that supports both static and animated images. GIFs rose to popularity as a way to react on social media without words.

Facebook and Twitter both now support GIFs. Giphy.com and tenor.com are a great place to start compiling your extensive archive of GIFs, sorted into folders by emotion.

Google Chrome: Google Chrome is a free web browser produced by Google that fully integrates with its online search system as well as its other applications.

Google Documents: Google Documents is a group of web-based office applications that includes tools for word processing, presentations, spreadsheet analysis, etc. All documents are stored and edited online and allow multiple people to collaborate on a document in real-time.

H.

Hashtag: A word or phrase preceded by the "#" sign. Hashtags are a simple way to mark the topic (or topics) of social media messages and make them discoverable to people with shared interests. On most social networks, clicking a hashtag will reveal recently published messages with that hashtag. Hashtags first emerged on Twitter as a user-created phenomenon and is now used on almost every other social media platform.

Header image: A header image refers to the large photo displayed at the top of your profile on Twitter. The header image is also commonly referred to as the banner image on LinkedIn or the cover image on Facebook.

Home: Often, the first page you see when you sign into your social media account. It contains a constantly updating timeline or feed of the user activity and news stories in your network.

I.

Impressions: An impression refers to a way in which marketers and advertisers keep track of every time an ad is "fetched" and counted.

Inbound marketing: A data-backed approach to attracting customers to web properties with relevant and helpful content. This content is discovered through channels like search engines and social media.

Influencer: A social media user with a significant audience who can drive awareness about a trend, topic, company, or product. From a marketer's perspective, the ideal influencer is also a passionate brand advocate. Successful influencer strategies usually involve the coordination of an organization's marketing, customer service, and public relations teams.

Influencer marketing: A strategy where a business collaborates with an influential person on social media to promote a product, service, or campaign. Think of it as micro-celebrity endorsements, designed for the digital age.

Instagram: A free online photo-sharing app that allows for the addition of several filters, editing, and sharing options.

Instant messaging (IM): A form of real-time, direct text-based communication between two or more people. More advanced instant messaging software clients also allow enhanced modes of communication, such as live voice or video calling.

K.

Key performance indicator (KPI): A metric that defines whether a marketing campaign or other initiative has succeeded or failed. KPIs for a social media marketing campaign might include brand mentions, replies, and retweets, or click-throughs to your website from individual posts.

L.

Like: Popularized digitally by Facebook—though derived from the dictionary definition—an understood expression of support for content. Along with shares, comments, and favorites, likes can be tracked as proof of engagement.

LinkedIn endorsement: A connection's recognition of another person's skill, such as content marketing, web programming, or cake baking. Endorsements, a form of social proof, boost your credibility through third-party confirmation that you have the skills you say you have. Users can endorse the skills of only their first-degree LinkedIn connections.

LinkedIn Publishing: LinkedIn's publishing platform functions as a place where members can publish long-form posts that relate to their professional interests and expertise. While this capability used to be limited to LinkedIn influencers only, the platform was opened to everyone in 2014.

LinkedIn SlideShare: An online social network for sharing presentations and documents. Users can favorite and embed presentations as well as share them on other social networks such as LinkedIn, Twitter, and Facebook.

LinkedIn recommendation: A written compliment from a connection that you can display on your LinkedIn profile to impress hiring managers, potential clients, and the 428 conference attendees you carpet-bombed with your business card. There's no limit to how many recommendations you can give or request, but remember that the most authentic recommendations come from people that you've worked with. If you receive a lackluster recommendation that you would rather not display, you can easily hide it from your profile. You can also edit, remove, or hide recommendations of your own LinkedIn connections at any time.

Listed: The act of being "listed" on Twitter refers to when a user curates a custom list of Twitter users to more easily keep tabs on their Tweets.

Live streaming: The act of delivering content over the Internet in real-time.

M.

Marketing automation: A combination of tactics and technology platforms that enable the automatic delivery of personalized content to prospects and customers through a variety of online channels. The idea behind marketing automation is giving website visitors and leads the information they need when they need it—and doing so at scale, which is where the automation comes in.

Marketing automation isn't about blindly scheduling content. Ideally, marketers will segment and score their marketing contacts, then nurture those potential customers with carefully tailored and timed messaging to move them toward an eventual purchase.

Solid social media marketing can attract new inbound leads, providing fuel for the marketing automation engine. Marketers can also make that engine more efficient by using social media data to learn more about their leads over time.

Mention: The act of tagging another user's handle or account name in a social media message. Mentions typically trigger a notification for that user and are a key part of what makes social media "social." A properly formatted mention also allows your audience to click through to the bio or profile of the user in question.

Messenger: An app that allows Facebook users to send one another instant messages through a smartphone. Facebook's Messenger app is now a necessity to access messages from mobile; users can no longer see their messages through a web browser.

Microblogging: Publishing smaller, more frequent quantities of content to platforms such as Twitter or Tumblr.

Multichannel attribution: An analytics tactic aimed at better understanding how customers discover, evaluate, and purchase your products or services.

When people buy products, they rarely complete a purchase in one step. For example, they might hear about a brand in a tweet, later see a banner ad for the product, then perform a Google search, and then, many days later, finally visit the website to purchase.

Multichannel attribution attempts to give relative value to each of these channels, treating each channel as a contributor to a customer's eventual purchase. The goal: to better understand the process by which your customers develop a holistic understanding of how each marketing channel.

N.

News feed: A news feed is a feed full of news. On Facebook, the News Feed is the homepage of users' accounts where they can see all the latest updates from their friends. The news feed on Twitter is called Timeline.

Notification: A message or update sharing new social media activity. For example, if somebody likes one of your Instagram photos you can receive a notification on your phone that lets you know.

O.

Omnichannel marketing: An approach to marketing that creates an integrated experience for audiences no matter what device they're using or which platform they use to interact with a brand.

Organic reach: The number of unique users who view your content without paid promotion. People find social content organically through their news feeds— either from companies whose pages they've liked themselves, or shared by friends or connections.

P.

Pay per click (PPC): Also known as cost per click (CPC), a type of advertising where an organization pays each time a user clicks on an advertisement. The costs incurred during a PPC campaign vary based on the competitiveness of the keyword phrase an organization is targeting with its ads.

Permalink: The URL of an individual piece of content. Permalinks allow you to directly reference a specific piece of content instead of searching for it in the feed or timeline where you found it. You can quickly find an item's permalink by clicking on its timestamp.

Phishing: An attempt to fraudulently acquire sensitive information such as usernames, passwords, or credit card information through authentic-looking electronic communication, usually email. Also, a method of spreading electronic viruses by exploiting security weaknesses.

Pinned Tweet: A Tweet that has been pinned to the top of a Twitter profile page. Pinning a Tweet is a great way to feature an important announcement—or that time you got retweeted so many times that you had to write a follow-up to promote your SoundCloud.

If your Tweets are public, anyone who views your profile page will see the Tweet.

Pin: Favorite links stored on Pinterest. Every Pin is made up of a picture and a description given by the user; when clicked, a Pin directs users to the source URL of the image. Other users can like or repin your Pins. Users can also organize Pins by theme or event into visual collections.

Pinterest: A visual organizer for saving and sharing links to sites and other media you like — also known as Pins. Pins are represented by an image and description of your choosing and organized into collections called Pinboards. Pinterest users can share their Pins with others, or repin pictures they liked from other users. Think of Pinterest as a virtual scrapbook, or a bookmarks page with pictures. Common uses include event planning, recipe collection, and fashion blogging — but savvy businesses across a spectrum of industries are learning to leverage this platform to grow their audience. Learn from these brands how to do it well.

Post: A social media status update, or an item on a blog or forum.

Promote Mode: A Twitter Ads feature that automatically promotes your first 10 tweets every day to a specified audience for a flat fee of $99 per month. Twitter estimates that accounts using Promote Mode will reach an average of 30,000 additional people.

Promoted Accounts: A Twitter Ads feature, announced in 2010, that invites targeted users to follow a certain account. This function is used to quickly grow a Twitter handle's following. Promoted accounts appear in users' timelines, Who to Follow suggestions, and search results.

Promoted Trends: A Twitter Ads feature that allows an advertiser to promote time, context, and event-sensitive trends to the top of the Trends list on Twitter. They are marked as "Promoted."

Promoted Tweets: Native advertisements targeted to a specific audience available through Twitter Ads. They look almost identical to organic Tweets in users' timelines but include a small "Promoted" marker. Promoted Tweets are used by advertisers to reach an expanded audience.

Protected: A private Twitter account. Only approved followers can view tweets and photos from a protected account or access their complete profile. Tweets from protected accounts cannot be natively retweeted, even by approved followers. (But even protected accounts should fear the dreaded screenshot.)

Q.

Quora: A Q&A website where anyone can ask their questions or answer other users' questions. For businesses, Quora can be a fantastic way to establish thought leadership or authority on a certain topic, or interact with users likely to be interested in their products or services.

R.

Reach: A data metric that determines the maximum potential audience for any given message. It is not a guarantee that the entire audience will see your social media post.

Reach is determined by a fairly complex calculation that includes number of followers, shares, and impressions, as well as net follower increase over time.

Real-time marketing: The practice of connecting with an online community around current events, trends, and customer feedback — often to a fault. If hopping on a hashtag bandwagon or personalizing a meme to your business isn't on the brand (ahem, dental offices still doing the Harlem Shake), it could fall flat with followers.

Recommendation: A term used to describe a written note from another LinkedIn member that aims to reinforce the user's professional credibility or expertise

Reddit: A popular social networking site where users upvote (positive) or downvote (negative) user-submitted content, from videos and image-based memes to text posts. The most upvoted and commented-on posts appear higher up on the website's main page, as well as on its many topic-focused sections called subreddits.

Regram: The act of reposting another Instagram user's image or video.

Reply: A Twitter action that allows a user to respond to a Tweet through a separate Tweet that begins with the other user's @username. This differs from a mention because Tweets that start with an @username only appear in the timelines of users who follow both parties.

Retargeting: An online advertising technique that aims to re-engage website visitors who left a site without converting. (If you've ever been followed around on the Internet by that pair of shoes you were drooling over during lunch, you've been retargeted.) Retargeting starts with a small tracking tag embedded in your website's code. Once visitors come to your website, you can then target them as they visit other websites, including search engines, social media sites, news outlets, and blogs.

The rationale is that these visitors are your best chance to make a sale, so instead of advertising to strangers, you spend your budget on prospects who have already visited your website.

Repin: To share another user's Pin on your own Pinterest Pinboard. To repin, simply hover over the Pin you love then select "repin." You can either add the Pin to an existing collection or start a new one. Like the Pin but don't want to a repin on it? Like it instead.

Reply: A response to someone's tweet. Unlike direct messages, replies are public.

Response rate: An engagement metric used to assess how much you are interacting with your social audience. To calculate your response rate, take the number of mentions that you have replied to in a given time period, and divide it by the total number of mentions you have received (excluding retweets).

Response volume: The total number of outbound messages that an organization, team, or specific social media account delivers in response to customer service issues within a given time.

Return on investment (ROI): It measures the gain or loss generated on an investment relative to the amount of money invested. ROI is usually expressed as a percentage and is typically used for personal financial decisions, to compare a company's profitability or to compare the efficiency of different investments.

Return on relationship (ROR): A measurement of the value gained by a person or business from developing a relationship. Measuring ROR isn't easy — it involves not only analyzing connection growth but also understanding the impact your customers' voices have on your brand and reputation. This includes sentiment analysis, as well as engagement metrics for your content, like organic sharing rates.

Retweet: A Tweet that is re-shared to the followers of another user's Twitter account. When you click the retweet button on the Twitter website or app, you can opt to republish the Tweet as is or add a comment to explain why you're sharing it or offer your hot take on the topic.

Rich pin: A Pinterest post that contains additional content. Rich Pins can be from one of four categories: app, article, recipe, or product. For example, product Rich Pins include real-time information about where to buy the product, pricing, and availability.

RSS: A format for syndicating web content (short for Rich Site Summary or Simple Syndication, depending on who you ask; neither is an official acronym). RSS feeds are created in a standard XML format that makes them compatible with a variety of readers and aggregators.

Content creators use RSS feeds to broadcast content (or content summaries) to audiences. Readers can subscribe to RSS feeds without providing personal information, and then automatically receive updates through a newsreader or aggregator. RIP Google Reader.

S.

Scheduling: Planning social media updates and content ahead of time, using a social relationship platform (SRP), or another publishing tool. Scheduling saves social professionals time in their daily workflows by allowing them to draft several messages at once, often as part of a publishing approval process. It also enables them to reach audiences in different time zones and organize extended marketing campaigns.

SEO: The practice of increasing the "organic" visibility of a web page in a search engine, such as Google. Although businesses can pay to promote their websites on search engine results pages (Search Engine Marketing or SEM), SEO refers to "free" tactics that enhance the search ranking of a page.

Share of voice: A measure of how many social media mentions a particular brand is receiving about its competition. Usually measured as a percentage of total mentions within an industry or among a defined group of competitors.

Shortlink: URL shortening is a technique on the World Wide Web in which a Uniform Resource

Locator (URL) may be made substantially shorter and still direct to the required page. This is achieved by using a redirect that links to the web page that has a long URL.

SlideShare: A popular social platform for sharing presentations and other business-oriented content. SlideShare makes it easy to embed content on websites and share it with other social networks, such as Facebook, Twitter, and LinkedIn (which has owned the platform since 2012).

Social commerce: An area of digital commerce where the buying process is assisted by social media and online networks.

Social listening: The process of finding and assessing what is being said about a company, topic, brand, or person on social media channels.

Social relationship platform: Secure, scalable technologies that allow businesses to manage social media communications of any kind across departments and devices. Think of a social relationship platform as a digital command and control: These tools put everything you need for social media in one place, making it easier to manage.

Social relationship platforms are used for monitoring, posting, and tracking social media, and help manage everything from customer service to lead generation. Hootsuite is a social relationship platform.

Social proof: Social proof refers to a psychological phenomenon in which people seek direction from those around them to determine how they are supposed to act or think in a given situation. In social media, social proof can be identified by the number of interactions a piece of content receives or the number of followers you have. The thought is that if others are sharing something or following someone, it must be good.

Social selling: The use of social media by sales professionals to increase productivity and generate revenue. Sellers can effectively leverage social media to enhance their reputations, expand their interpersonal networks, and attract new prospects. They can also identify buyers by listening and engaging in the online spaces where potential customers are conducting research and asking for advice.

StumbleUpon: StumbleUpon is a free web browser extension that acts as an intelligent browsing tool for discovering and sharing web sites.

Spam: Unnecessary and repetitive content that clogs up in boxes and clutters social media feeds. In other words, the bane of your existence.

Sponsored posts: Content on a social media site that has been paid for by a brand or organization. Every social media platform has its form of sponsored content; brands can leverage sponsored content to get visibility with a larger audience that might be interested in their messages, products, or services.

T.

Tag: A keyword added to a social media post with the original purpose of categorizing related content. You can also tag someone in a post or photo, which creates a link to their social media profile and associates them with the content. Many services also offer the option to remove unwanted tags from your profile.

Terms of service: The rules individuals must follow to use a product or service. Every social platform has a detailed set of terms of service (ToS for short) that you agree to when creating a profile; if at any point you violate those terms, you can be banned from the service or have your account deleted. Users should take care to understand the agreements they sign when joining a social media site, including the terms of service and privacy policy; these documents are legally binding contracts.

Thread: A string of messages that make up a conversation. Threads begin with an initial message and then continue as a series of replies or comments.

Threads are essential to most forms of online communication, including social media and email.

Without them, it's extremely ifficult to keep track of ongoing conversations (see also: pre-2013 Facebook, or email before Gmail).

Timestamp: The date and time that a message is posted to a social network, usually visible near the post's title or corresponding username. Clicking on a timestamp will usually bring you to the content's permalink.

Top Tweets: The most popular and engaging tweets for a given search query, as determined by a Twitter algorithm. Searches on Twitter's website return top Tweets by default, or you can toggle to "All" results to see the full list of matching Tweets.

Trend, trending: A topic or hashtag that is popular on social media at a given moment. Trends are highlighted by social networks such as Twitter and Facebook to encourage discussion and engagement among their users. The "trending" concept was first popularized by Twitter and has since been adopted by Facebook and other networks. The trends that you see on Twitter and Facebook are personalized for you, based on your location, who you follow, and the content you like.

Triage: The process of prioritizing, assigning, and responding to inbound social media messages. The term is borrowed from emergency medicine, where it is crucial to assess the relative urgency of every case to prioritize care.

In a social media triage process, incoming messages are filtered, evaluated for urgency, assigned to the necessary parties, and, if necessary, escalated so that the organization can provide the appropriate response (either online, offline, or both).

Troll: A social media user who makes a deliberately offensive or annoying posting with the sole aim of provoking other users.

Tumblr: A microblogging platform that allows users to post text, images, video, audio, links, and quotes to their blog. Users can also follow other blogs and repost other users' content to their blog.

Tweet: A Twitter message. Tweets are limited to 280 characters of text (including URLs) and could include embedded photos, videos, and some other forms of media. They are public by default and will show up in Twitter timelines and searches unless they are sent from protected accounts or as direct messages. Tweets can also be embedded in website pages.

Need more than 280 characters to get your message across? Hit the + button below your post to add an additional threaded tweet, then publish them all together.

Twitter list: A personalized, curated collection of Twitter accounts. On public accounts, lists are visible to all users, and users can follow other users' lists if desired. Users can see a feed of Tweets from just one list's accounts by clicking the name of the list.

Twitter Moments: Twitter Moments are curated stories about what's happening around the world — powered by Tweets. It's easy to create your own story with Twitter Moments.

U.

URL: Short for Uniform Resource Locator, the location of a website page, or other resources on the Internet.

URL shortener: A tool that condenses a URL into a shorter (and more social media-friendly) format. Users who click on a short link are redirected to the original web address. URL shorteners, such as Bitly or ow.ly, can also provide link tracking capabilities, which allow businesses to measure click-throughs from social media and attribute website conversions to individual social messages.

User-generated content: Media that has been created and published online by the users of a social or collaboration platform, typically for non-commercial purposes. User-generated content is one of the defining characteristics of social media.

Many companies have enthusiastically embraced and encouraged user-generated content as a means of increasing brand awareness and customer loyalty. User-generated campaigns (such as Instagram contests) allow businesses to tap into the creative energies of their customers and use the contributions to fuel ongoing marketing tactics.

V.

Vanity URL: A web address that is branded for marketing purposes. Vanity URLs are customized to replace common URL shortener formats with something more closely related to an organization's branding. For example, instead of ow.ly or bit.ly, Time Inc.'s vanity URL is ti.me. The New York Times uses nyti.ms.

Verified: An account whose owner has proven their identity with the social media platform provider. This is usually reserved for brands, journalists, and other public figures as a way of preventing fraud and protecting the integrity of the person or organization behind the account.

Views: In reference to Snapchat, these are users who have looked at your Snap Story. To see who has viewed their story, users simply need to click the eye symbol next to their Story.

Viral: A term used to describe an instance in which a piece of content - YouTube video, blog article, photo, etc. - achieves noteworthy awareness. Viral distribution relies heavily on word of mouth and the frequent sharing of one particular piece of content all over the Internet.

Vlogger: Someone who creates and broadcasts video blogs.

W.

Webinar: A portmanteau of the word's "website" and "seminar," a digital broadcast of a presentation intended to educate or inform. Webinars allow users to see or hear a presentation from their computer or other devices and often interact directly with the presenter or fellow attendees through chat or video.

YouTube: Can be used as a noun to describe the website on which users upload, store, and share videos, or as a verb to describe the practice of consuming/creating content from/for the website

References

Buffa, J. (2013, February 13). *Cisco.* Retrieved from https://blogs.cisco.com/socialmedia/youtube-and-the-customer-journey?dtid=osscdc000283

Collier, A. (2019). *Contant Contact .* Retrieved from https://blogs.constantcontact.com/why-social-media-marketing/#

Corona, B. (2018, Feburary). Retrieved from https://www.bluecorona.com/blog/local-seo-nap-consistency-guide

Heing, I. (2018, June). *The State of Tech.* Retrieved from https://themanifest.com/social-media/7-reasons-consider-paid-social-media-advertising

Hootsuite . (n.d.). Retrieved from https://hootsuite.com/pinterest

Hubspot. (n.d.). Retrieved from https://www.hubspot.com/youtube-marketing

MacDonald, J. (2017, May). *Business 2 Community .* Retrieved from https://www.business2community.com/social-media/importance-hashtags-know-use-01837644

Pinkham, R. (2019). *Constant Contact .* Retrieved from https://blogs.constantcontact.com/what-is-linkedin/

readyartwork. (n.d.). Retrieved from https://www.readyartwork.com/business-video-marketing-strategy/

Readyartwork . (n.d.). Retrieved from https://www.readyartwork.com/business-video-marketing-strategy/

Shaw, B. (2019). *SEO Expert .* Retrieved from https://seoexpertbrad.com/dominate-local-seo-marketing/

Small Business . (n.d.). Retrieved from https://www.sba.gov/sites/default/files/March_April_2016_FINAL_508_compliant.pdf

Small Business Administration . (n.d.). Retrieved from https://www.sba.gov/

US Small Business Administration. (n.d.). Retrieved from
https://www.sba.gov/sites/default/files/FAQ_March_2014
_0.pdf

Author Bio

 Writers Publishing House/Ghost Writer Media is a solid publishing firm with more than a decade of assisting clients with their publishing needs. Founder and Owner Lizzy McNett understands the importance of exemplary customer service; it is the basis for any successful business. She believes, "Everyone should profit from their passion."

Lizzy writes books, which makes perfect sense considering her website. She is best known for ghostwriting biographies/business books of various genres, along with her novels based on the initial part of her working career, horse training.

When not absorbed in writing for clients, Lizzy can be found hiking, biking, or any outside activity. Although she does not train horses anymore, their spirits will always be part of her soul. She had a BA in fine arts, with a minor in Equine Science, and studied at Scottsdale Art Institute under Robert 'Shoofly' Shufelt.

If you're ready to tell "Your Story", please visit her website at writerspublishinghouse.com, where you can contact Lizzy about starting your book project today. "What's Your Story?"

Lizzy McNett, BA
CEO, Writers Publishing House, ICOMM4U.CO

An Expert In Developing Exceptional Processes To Brand Best-Selling Authors

Lizzy's Bio:
Literary Agent | Amazon International #1Bestselling Author | Business/Marketing Speaker | 18 Years' Publishing Expert BA, Fine Arts | Entrepreneur

Anna's Books: annaelizabethjudd.com

- The Power of Thought
- IAuthor – Social Media Marketing Guide
- ICOMM – Conservative Business/Marketing Guide
- The Broken Angel – A Guide to Self-Realization

- The Handbook of Horsemanship
- The Broncobusters
- The Hourglass of el Diablo

- Marshal Spur and the Outlaw
- The Boy Who Couldn't Talk
- Spur Up! – Music Album
- Hey, Hay Learn Your ABC's
- Learn Your ABCs with Haystack

- A Distant Calling
- Skimmer's Adventure